Dodging Coconuts

How to Survive the Storm and Rebuild Your Life

Sylvia Lovely

Grassy Creek Publishing
Lexington, KY

Grassy Creek Publishing
2293 Savannah Lane
Lexington, Kentucky 40513

This is a business memoir based on the author's best recollections and on public records in the form of newspaper articles, letters, and other factual resources.

Ordering Information: Bulk sales and special discounts are available on quantity purchases by schools, corporations, associations, and others. For details, contact Sylvia@SylviaLovely.com_at the address above. To have Ms. Lovely speak to your group you can contact her by email at Sylvia@SylviaLovely.com.

Dodging Coconuts/Sylvia Lovely -- 1st Ed.
ISBN 978-0-9975338-0-4
ISBN Electronic 978-0-9975338-1-4
Library of Congress 2016940751
Business Memoir

MIKE GOBB

1963 - 2013

This book is dedicated to the memory of Michael Arthur Gobb—we loved him like a brother. He was beautiful.

"As time passed, my father struggled for more to hold onto, asking me again and again: had I told him everything. Finally, I said to him, maybe all I know about Paul is that he was a fine fisherman. You know more than that, my father said; he was beautiful. And that was the last time we spoke of my brother's death."

—from the novel *A River Runs Through It*, by *Norman Maclean*

If it all ended tomorrow, I know that I have lived a charmed life. However, along the way, something happened that was more than a hiccup in my life plan. Near the end of a highly successful twenty-five-year career, I was "fired." It was shocking and unbelievable to me and to my friends and colleagues. It was a confluence of events: a crushing Great Recession that pushed the reset button on the world, a media that was crashing and burning, information overload, wrongdoing by an airport director, and missed signals by me.

What happened to me, and to others dear to me, broke my heart. I fell fast and hard from being the "darling" of the press to being branded with a "scarlet letter" of shame. Afterward, I descended into a deep depression, which affected my health and caused my family and friends to worry. They wondered, so they tell me now, if I would ever recover. Like too many others, I had become wedded to life in the fast lane. I had lost track of what was truly important to a fulfilled life and missed the warning signals. When midnight struck on my Cinderella-life, I realized that I had let my career and other people define my success and my failure. When "it" happened, I did not know what to do or where to turn.

Only months after I was "fired." I suffered a

medical catastrophe that has resulted in permanent health problems. Following that was the suicide of my good friend Mike Gobb. I did not realize that what happened to me was a gift: the gift of self-reflection.

While reading the newspaper one day, I discovered Richard Pulga's story of the coconuts, and the impetus for this book was born.

What I learned from my experience is that we will all have "storms" in our lives. Some are expected. Some are not. They may come in the form of an illness, a death, or a sudden career setback. Are you ready? Would you know what to do, and how to protect yourself and your loved ones? Would you know how to take evasive action? That is what this book is all about—learning how to react appropriately and calmly to an unexpected or an impending career, life, or reputation disaster.

The coconuts are flying all around; it is not "if" they will strike, but "when." The hit is random. It can happen to anyone. Once caught in a set of circumstances, you must take control of the situation or it will certainly take control of you.

What I Learned:

- Understand that "Success" does not necessarily mean you are living a balanced life. There is a difference between your real life with family and friends and your career-life. I thought, before the reputation disaster, that I was a grand success. It turns out; I was not successful in the ways that mattered.

- Know who your real friends are. I found out quickly how many "friends" I had by the phone calls that were suddenly unanswered.
- Focus on your *Purpose:* that inner guiding light of strength that will be there no matter what happens.
- Be *Prepared* by knowing the micro and macro forces of the world around you.
- Develop a contingency *Plan* for handling what might happen.
- Recognize that you must develop the *Perspective of Leadership,* which will enable you to handle the flying coconuts with a bigger catcher's mitt.
- Embrace leadership, which is a mix of humility and hutzpah. Stand up and be counted to defend the truth and take responsibility.
- Know that humor provides the salve that gets you through difficult times.

When my disasters struck, I was not prepared and had no contingency plan. I simply threw up my hands when the bus pulled out in front of me. I did not speak up and defend my organization or myself. Nor did I assume responsibility for what needed to change. I simply went underground into depression. I listened to conventional wisdom on how to react. I did not realize how much the world had changed. Many forces that I could not control were at play. I missed many signals that could have protected my organization and me. Others lived my story with me and shared the same stage; my husband Bernie Lovely and Mike Gobb, the former CEO of a regional airport.

Mike and I were highly accomplished CEOs, well respected in our roles; Bernie was also the volunteer chair of the airport board, which is a typical role for a highly regarded attorney. I was the CEO of the Kentucky League of Cities (KLC). It all takes place in the rolling bluegrass hills of Central Kentucky. The lessons of our experiences are timeless and not bound by geography or job descriptions. We were hit simultaneously with a stealth strike that none of us saw coming. We should have.

We were successful ... until we were not. Our lives were forever altered by related and intertwined events, caused by a confluence of cultural and economic forces.

Sometimes in life, the questions are more important than the answers: What could I have done differently? What could I have done better? What is the boundary of forgiveness for those involved in a set of circumstances that in some instances we could have controlled? These are hard questions, which required taking responsibility for my recovery and myself. They entailed much reflection and meditation to answer.

Many of my friends say that I could have done nothing to change the outcome of what happened to me. I believed that for a long time. With time and reflection, I have changed my mind. It has been six years since my reputation and health disasters and Mike's suicide. In those intervening years, I have learned many things. The number-one revelation is that disasters come with hidden gifts … if we are willing to embrace them.

My gift to you is the experience of having survived the crisis, and come out of it stronger and with a deep appreciation for life.

No matter *where* you are on life's path, you must pause and take stock of *who* you are.

- Hold firm to the core of your own *Purpose* through simple self-examination.
- Be *Prepared* by understanding the micro and macro forces in our rapidly changing world.
- *Plan* your life in a way that provides balance between your work life and your personal life.
- Understand that when the pieces of setbacks lie before you like shattered glass, you can add the uniquely human quality of *Perspective* and move on.

So, what can you do when the universe has seemingly singled you out? Do you hide under the covers or do you tease through the wreckage and cobble together a life lesson or two that can help others?

     I choose the latter. That is why I wrote this book.

Sylvia Lovely

THE PARABLE OF THE COCONUTS

On a November day in 2013, I came upon an article in the *New York Times*[1] about a young man who died from a broken leg. The article was entitled "Death after the Typhoon: It Was Preventable," written by Keith Bradshaw.

> "Richard Pulga lay on a hard steel gurney for five days with only a saline drip after being seriously injured in the typhoon that devastated his country. On the fifth day Mr. Pulga, 27, died—essentially of a broken leg."

Richard Pulga was struck by a flying coconut, which shattered his leg. He died five days later, essentially of a broken leg, which should never have ended his life.

He lived with his family in Tacloban, the Philippines. He thought he had made all the necessary preparations for the onslaught of the coming storm—Typhoon Haiyan.

He was only 27, the father of two small children, and one of the few members of his extended family able to earn a meager living. He had taken all the precautions he knew to take. He had moved his family to a safe place while he stayed with the farm, tied down loose things so they would not fly around, and covered what he could. He had forgotten one thing: the coconuts. He lived with them every day, taking them for granted. He ate their

---

[1] *New York Times, "Death after the typhoon: It was preventable";* Bradshaw, Keith; November 15, 2013.

nourishing meat and drank the liquid inside the hard shells.

He never imagined that the coconuts would become flying missiles of destruction in the storm.

> "By the time Dr. Rodel Flores, a surgeon with a team of visiting doctors, found Mr. Pulga, he had received no antibiotics or antiseptic and his leg was badly infected. The doctor ordered an emergency amputation to try to save his life. But the surgery was too late, and death soon followed. 'In short, his death was preventable,' said Dr. Flores."

The loss was catastrophic. Mr. Pulga was a subsistence farmer and the sole breadwinner for his family. His grieving widow, Jennifer, kept a vigil beside his body.

This made me think about my own "typhoon," one followed quickly by two medical disasters. Could Mr. Pulga have altered the course of his fate, or I, mine.

Should he have taken the more cautious view, abandoned the farm, and fled with his family?

Should he have known that coconuts could, through external forces beyond our control, become weapons of destruction?

Did he realize that, ultimately, he was to battle the storm and its aftermath alone? The government failed utterly in providing medicine and necessary medical personnel.

In the midst of the storm, Mr. Pulga was alone—left to his own resources.

His story did not have to end this way. Had the government been more prepared, or had he, it might have turned out differently.

We live our lives within the boundaries of our gifts and limitations, take reasonable precautions, and are aware of the power of storms that can blow up and wreck our surroundings. However, "the perfect storm" can catch any of us off-guard.

You did not see it coming. The coconuts hit you hard. Now your life depends on what actions you take, or do not take. Could you have prepared for the unexpected ferocity of the storm? Could you have understood that, in the crucible, no one was going to be there to rescue you? Did you know that you needed to live with the knowledge that the coconuts could come flying at any moment?

Watch for the signs—be aware, and never assume that things *are* as they appear. Realize that which seems ordinary and harmless can become lethal.

At some point in our lives, or in our careers, or both, some of us will experience the "perfect storm" or perhaps a lesser crisis. This book is about being prepared, ahead of time, for that eventuality.

"One day I would be a better hand at the game. One day I would learn how to laugh."

—From the novel *Steppenwolf,* by Hermann Hesse

CHAPTER ONE

A Good Girl

"A crucible is a container made of metal for heating substances to high temperatures to the point that they change shape."

—Webster's Collegiate Dictionary

In modern times, a crucible has come to mean a severe, searching test. This term, *crucible*, popularized in Arthur Miller's play by the same name, is the story of the Salem witch trials that took place in Massachusetts Bay in 1692 and 1693. It became an allegoric reference to the McCarthyism of the early 1950s, when the U.S. government blacklisted suspected communists. The blacklisting resulted in shattered careers and lives.

We all face a crucible at some point. We never know how we will be tested or how that test will change us. According to writer Sarah Desson in her book, *The Truth about Forever:* "Grief can be a burden, but also an anchor. You get used to the weight, how it holds you in place. It is best to learn how to cope and build resilience as the counter to what has and may come."

The crucible is random. Surviving one test provides no guarantee another will not come your way. It is better to learn how to avoid, field, and ultimately handle each crucible and find peace in knowing you did your best.

August 2009

I was "fired" from my dream job on August 19, 2009. "They" called it retirement, but make no mistake, I was fired. I had held my CEO position for more than twenty years, and had received much praise—not only from my governing board members, but also from others around the country who were aware of and involved with my work. I lost not only my dream job, but also nearly my life as I sank into deep depression. It did not have to end this way.

Much had preceded my crucible. It involved Bernie, my husband, and Mike Gobb, who was the executive director of a central-Kentucky regional airport. In all my years of knowing the actors who appeared in the midst of the chaos late in my career, I would never have guessed their ultimate roles and the twists and turns that would occur.

It is my heartfelt belief that my story and those of Bernie and Mike are woven together by fact and by cosmic coincidence. However, to different degrees, the same forces of economic distress, political theater, human weakness, and missteps affected us all.

None of us arrived at the crucible in a vacuum. Like everyone else, we were the product of our experiences, our upbringings, and chance encounters with those who have become our friends or foes. All those experiences visit us when the crucible arrives, and the universe does not distinguish between the deserving and the undeserving.

Stephen Crane's words in *War is Kind and Other Poems* begins with, "Sir, I exist"; so does the universe reply: "that does not create an obligation in me."[2] As I often observe, you never know. You truly do not.

Before the crucible, I was a success story out of nineteenth-century author Horatio Alger, who wrote "rags to riches" stories, in which one rises above poverty to become successful through hard work, determination, courage, and honesty.

I was born to parents with few resources or opportunities; however, they believed in the American Dream that their children's lives could be better than their own. My parents grew up in the Appalachian foothills or "hollers" of Morgan County, Kentucky. "Hollers" are the gaps between the unforgiving mountains that limited traditional development, including an economy that created

---

[2] *War is Kind and Other Poems*, published June 19, 1998.

jobs. My ancestors were part of the migration of east-coasters across the Appalachian chain and into these lush and shrouded lands.

I surmise that my Irish and Scottish ancestors who first landed on the Atlantic shore were likely the poorest of the poor, who potato and other famines chased from the homeland—the unwanted migrants of their day. They were strong-willed, burnished by their hard life that produced an independent streak.

This heritage led me to observe three kinds of Kentuckians from that era: those who left for the factories of the North, like my parents; those who stayed behind and worked at odd jobs or collected "government" checks; and those who left or stayed, but were lucky and/or connected enough to start entrepreneurial ventures. In any case, the streak of independence and "gumption" came shining through.

Life for me was different from that of my parents. My life was a series of "happy accidents" that always turned out right. Others opened doors for me. I raced through those doors, propelled by a healthy dose of ambition. My parents' hardscrabble life fueled a determination in me to escape their fate. I would seize every opportunity that came my way. I had gumption.

My Parents

My father was one of ten children, and my mother one of seven. Big families were the norm in rural Appalachia. Appalachian children tilled the patches of available flat land and found work here and there, but—for the most part—were as poor as church mice. As my father put it, "We got one pair of shoes in the winter— sometimes used, and maybe an orange for Christmas."

His family was luckier than most. "We killed a hog in November, hung it in the smoke-house, and ate vegetables grown in the garden Mammy (his mother) would can." Canning was an annual neighborhood ritual in the early fall, with pots of scalding water ensuring the winter's supply. Some lucky families eked out sufficient flat land for a small base of tobacco, which could make the difference in eating or going hungry.

According to my father, "We ate well and played checkers with our neighbors." To his death, he was an excellent checkers player, though he offered that his sister Grace was even better. Front porches in the holler were active places and, if the crops were good, food was ample. "Checkers tourneys" lasted for days.

I have seen pictures of my parents, in their early twenties, in the midst of courtship. My mother is hiding her shy smile, while my father projects a broad, happy grin. Early pictures provide clues to later life. As long as I knew her, my mother was unhappy—never feeling that she measured up to others; I discovered antidepressants among her medications after her death. My father, on the other hand, was always content. He believed he had done the best he could with what he had. My mother passed away at age 74; my father died at 92.

Daddy quit school after the death of his father to care for siblings. "How old was my grandfather when he died?" I asked.

"In his forties ... I guess. Daddy got sick. He kept losing weight and grew weak ... and then he died."

"Did you take him to the doctor, Daddy? What was his diagnosis? What was his treatment?" My father looked at me as if I had suggested that he go to the moon and back.

With a chuckle he replied, "We didn't go to doctors back then. We had no money and no insurance." That was before safety nets like Medicaid and Medicare.

My parents followed the path of many thousands of Kentuckians who went to work in the factories of the Midwest. They left Kentucky in 1948, when Daddy found work at the National Cash Register (NCR) Company in Dayton, Ohio. It was a time when he could make a decent middle-class living with an eighth-grade education.

It took courage to load a pickup truck and move to a future far removed from the green, peaceful hills of eastern Kentucky, to the drab Dayton area, filled with concrete factory buildings. Of course, my parents were not alone. Many fled for the plentiful jobs and settled in little Kentucky Diasporas spread across the Midwest.

My mother followed a typical pattern of her era and stayed at home with my brother and me. After we left home, she went to work as an elementary school custodian, which made her proud. Working and earning money were important goals for my mother, probably because she had so little growing up. She would tell stories about going to work, so that younger children in the family could remain in school.

Working gave her a sense of pride. Near the time of her death, at the age of 74, she entrusted me with her precious Social Security card. Going through her belongings after her death, I discovered a number of fast-food-employment applications. She had been caring for my boys as they grew to be teenagers. The job applications must have been for "after" her babysitting job was finished. She was determined to work and always have money coming in. I inherited that trait.

My brother, Keith, was born after my parents moved to Dayton. Although I never knew why, they moved back to Kentucky after Keith's birth for one more try at farming, their first love. This time, they settled on a rented farm close to their birthplace where Interstate 64 now cuts through. I joke that I was the straw that broke the camel's back and was the cause of my parents' final return to Ohio in 1951.

I was born in Frenchburg, Kentucky, in November 1950, during one of the worst winters on record. My father told stories about how he wrapped his truck tires with rags to cross the snowy mountain to the tiny hospital founded by the Presbyterian Church as a part of its mission to provide medical and educational services to poor regions. When he came for my mother and me the next day, the nurse admonished him not to take us out into the snow and cold so soon. In tortured English, he replied, "I don't have no money; I don't have no insurance. I'm taking them home."

My father got his old job back at NCR upon returning in 1951. Numerous men were vying for every opening, and he had after all voluntarily left just a year before to return to Kentucky. "I went to the personnel office, and they told me I had to go to my old foreman–Sibya (my nick- name). I didn't walk; I ran to see old Gudgel, and he told me to come back on the job that evening."

"Congratulations on a job well done," he seemed to say. Grinning, he was giving himself a big verbal "pat on the back" for having accomplished what may have appeared to be a next-to-impossible task.

My father worked at NCR as a drill press operator until the late 1970s, when—as he described it— "computers put me out of work." I never knew what a drill press operator did, but I can imagine rows of machines rat-a-tatting and spitting out tiny cogs that were part of what made up a cash register. The employment test was how many tiny pieces a prospective employee could turn each hour. My father was fast, which qualified him for continued employment and raises.

Thousands of workers just like my dad toiled in the barrack-like buildings, producing a peak of 110,000 cash registers in one year. Though drab, they were places of hope and belief in the future for the many expatriate Kentuckians. My father loved NCR and never tired of telling how kind the company was to its workers. I remember his delight at the announcement that workers would be given their birthday off with pay.

Just prior to his death in 2013, I took my 92-year-old father to the Carillon Historical Park museum next to the place where the factory had stood. I had hoped that the curators, who were collecting oral histories of the former

NCR workers, would interview him. It was too late. Dementia had set in. However, upon visiting a room devoted to cash registers in honor of NCR and the workers, my father came alive with delight.

The entire room was filled with vintage cash registers produced at the factory and representing the different models churned out over the years. Like General Motors cars of the forties and fifties they were big, flashy, and— no doubt in their day—something of a status symbol. This room could have been an arcade, casino hall … or a brothel.

Following the timeline from the beginning to obsolescence, they became less gaudy and more drab and "corporate" in appearance. Of course, computers and even iPads have replaced cash registers. Perhaps that is why Steve Jobs has been so successful with Apple devices. He intuitively understood our hardwired need for beauty.

My father bought his clothing at garage sales. Throughout my adult life, he would quiz me about how much I spent. I never told him the true price. As a little girl, I was hardwired to halve the price of any dress my mother and I bought. "Better that way," said my mother, "otherwise he will worry."

Though born in the hills and hollers, I grew up in Ohio and enjoyed a solid middle-class up-bringing. Until he was laid-off, my father worked any shift—day or night as requested. He once expressed that he was lucky to have kept his job until we were through school. My full-time job was "school," and my parents were taskmasters at making sure I kept my eye on the ball.

The only times I can recall being scolded for sloppy schoolwork or poor grades (neither of which happened often) was in the fourth-grade. A violin teacher came to my school: Fairborn Elementary. Fairborn was located about twelve miles outside Dayton, which might as well have been 300 miles. Fairborn was a small town in every way.

Playing the violin felt as natural as breathing to me, and I excelled. I became obsessed to the exclusion of all else. I remember a stern scolding when I brought home an F in science, which was not my usual A.

My precious violin was soon banished to the basement, when my teacher moved away and my parents steadfastly refused to drive me to Dayton to find another. They were likely relieved of the burden of understanding my strange fascination with the violin. "Practical" piano lessons took its place. My parents explained, "You can play piano in church."

Church plays an outsized role in those with Appalachian roots. Maybe this life of deprivation encouraged the thought that things and places were better "on the other side." To this day, my music taste runs to mournful tunes of the genre reflecting life in the Appalachian hills, such as the artistry of Gillian Welch:

> *We can't have all things to please us*
> *No matter how hard we try*
> *Until we've all gone to Jesus,*

we can only wonder why.[3]

In rummaging through old photos and memorabilia, I found numerous certificates of achievement earned throughout school. I recall vying for and achieving "first chair" (the teachers would literally move children around in the room according to grades received on tests) in a number of subject areas, particularly in history and science. I remember buying Scientific American magazine when I was just a girl. While I am rarely the smartest person in the room, I am unnaturally curious, and possess a love of knowing and learning things.

Early on, I had no awareness of the bias against Kentuckians, or that I lacked the connections and the polish of my peers. We were different. Poking fun at transplanted Kentuckians for their attachment to family "back home" and their backward ways was common. "Do you leave your shoes at the Ohio River when you go home on the weekend?" schoolmates would ask and then regale us with their laughter.

Despite my good grades and high test-scores, I was enrolled in a special secretarial program.

I was undaunted. In my senior year of high school, I announced a desire to go to college. I loved learning, so this was a natural leap.

My parents were shocked, but delighted. Paying attention to my grades was one thing, but COLLEGE?

---

[3] From the song, "Annebelle"; Welch, Gillian; lyrics by Welch, Gillian.

They must have pinched themselves in disbelief, as this must have seemed unreachable and unthinkable.

After a brief showdown over "going away to school," they relented and agreed to let me pursue my dream of independence. There was but one condition—I had to attend Morehead State University, a regional university located in the heart of Appalachia, back home in their beloved Kentucky.

At college, I was the turnip that fell off the truck. However, MSU was well versed in the care, feeding, development and the "magic" of turning a freshman "sow's ear" into a senior "silk purse." MSU is often the first-choice college of high school graduates like me—first-generation college students with roots in Appalachia—rough around the edges, but bursting with ambition and potential. One of my treasured board assignments was serving on both the MSU Board of Regents and years later, serving as its chair. It was quite a meteoric rise, given my humble beginnings. I possessed gumption, if anything.

Whether it was a dinner event at a local restaurant or the Miss MSU Pageant, in which I inexplicably found myself in the top-ten contestants, my raw-as-a-corncob nature always shone through. It was as if my destiny reminded me of how poorly I fit into the world. It was a world in which I craved inclusion.

I never stopped trying. "I'll have that super salad," I responded to the server who asked if I wanted "soup or salad" at a dinner party with my professors and other students. Awkward silence met my gaff. Up to that point in my life, eating out consisted of the Big Boy Restaurant in Ripley, Ohio. We ate there, just before we would cross the Ohio River into Kentucky, heading to my grandmother's house in Morgan County.

Another moment was the MSU pageant, which sent my mother and me off in a panic to acquire the clothes befitting an appearance on stage with some attractive, "pulled together" young women. I cannot for the life of me know why I made the top ten, except that I was told my talent performance made the difference—or shall I say my "made-up" talent. With panic as the mother of invention, I "invented" a performance based on thirteen years of piano lessons that had yielded little in the way of playing the instrument. Was it my deep-seated resentment and rebellion at having to give up my beloved violin? I had even attempted to major in piano—an inexplicable choice given my profound inability to play. My tearful piano teacher broke that news to me early on.

I have always believed that great musicians possess confidence. They know about singing and playing like no one is listening, and dancing as if no one is watching. Like my parents, I lacked self-confidence and suffered from a nagging sense that I did not deserve to "fit" into the world in which I found myself. Whatever the answer, I had to come up with a talent performance fast. What do you do if you cannot do anything else? I developed a comedy routine, depicting a little girl who tries to memorize—but cannot remember—her music at the annual piano recital. That had happened to me during more than one dismal recital experience.

On stage the night of the pageant, I received applause and accolades. I loved it. It was exhilarating. I cannot remember much of what happened afterward, except that I did not win or even make the final cut. I do know that I enjoyed the stage and performing comedy. Perhaps comedy allowed me the outlet to poke fun at myself.

I switched my major to English and excelled. I met and married Bernie just prior to my senior year. That was to prove a blessing because we came from similar backgrounds and, in fits and starts, grew up together.

CHAPTER TWO

Bernie and Mike

"Accept the things to which fate binds you, and love the people with whom fate brings you together, but do so with all your heart."

—Marcus Aurelius

Bernie

Bernie's life mirrored my own, but was different in one significant way. He was born into a family of tinkerers, which was a common "profession" in the eastern Kentucky Mountains. Today, such a professional bent

Unlike my father, who was a follower, Big Bernie was a leader. In addition to ministering, he was elected to the city council in Harlan. Outsiders are not easily embraced in Appalachia. Big Bernie was different. He served as a role model and mentor for thousands of young people in his churches.

His last assignment before retiring was pastoring a church in Morehead, Kentucky. He also served in elected office as a county magistrate. When he died, record crowds came to his funeral to pay their respects.

Because of the leadership qualities that he no doubt inherited from his dad, my Bernie became the North Star of my life. In one respect, he was unlike his father. His strength reflected a quieter nature. Yet, he was calm and steady; perhaps a reactionary stance against his father's boisterous and outgoing ways. He had the same strength of character. Today, we joke that he is a counselor, not as a lawyer—which is his profession—but of the kind that people, including our two boys and a host of others, seek out in moments of crisis.

He was steady, where I was impetuous. He was contented, where I was anything but. He had the strengths of an entrepreneur, but the steadiness that bespoke the contemplative life of a college professor, a position to which he once aspired. His "nature" complimented mine … including my tendency to strike out in any direction. We were both unaware of and unprepared for the world we would enter.

Born in 1948, Bernie came of age in the tumultuous years of student uprisings. It was a tense time and campus unrest was the news of the day. It was on May 4, 1970, that the tragic Kent State shootings took place, resulting in the deaths of four student protesters.

Bernie was a hippie. Named after the familiar "hipsters" and beatniks of earlier days, hippies had an irreverent attitude toward dress and other conventions. The movement was antiestablishment and anti-corporate. He adopted liberal causes, grew his hair long, and participated in student government at Morehead, while working on a master's degree in English literature. Bernie chose that major due to his interest in the activist writers of the day and, as he would say, "It was anything but a business degree."

I was just the opposite—not at all political and desperately trying to fit into the "in" crowd. I became an honorary little sister of a fraternity—something for which all the cute girls vied. I was accepted by a social sorority, in a competitive process, but backed out because my parents could not afford the dues. Though they agreed to let me join, my guilt would not allow it. My mother would tell me stories about how my father trembled as the nightly news reported the NCR layoffs according to seniority. He knew he would lose his job; he just did not know when. He was desperate to hold on until I got through college.

I met Bernie during my junior year. As an English major, I had little sense of direction. Because I loved literature and reading, I auditioned to serve on the board of

the MSU literary magazine, Inscape. Because I was mi-
noring in music, I was not the usual candidate. In addition, I lived in the "sorority dorm," despite not being a
member of a social sorority. I had become a member of a
music fraternity, Sigma Alpha Iota, which was technically
a "fraternity" because it was educational in nature. That
fraternity was in the sorority dorm. My residence status
would later come into play.

Upon arriving at the audition before the board
members, I mentally noted that they looked like the
scruffy members of an acid rock band—the Jimmy Hen-
dricks-Rolling Stones "alternative" rock band look so in
vogue in the early seventies. I, on the other hand, was
boringly traditional. I could sense the skepticism of the
board. Bernie, handsome and roguish, was a member.

I submitted a writing sample. While I have no recol-
lection of what I submitted or of its quality, I suspect I
was selected not because I was a great writer, but because
Bernie was smitten with me. I later learned that he asked
me out on a date only after being assured that I was not a
"sorority girl," even though I lived in "that" dorm.

He picked me up for our first date at the library. (I
was a prodigious studier.) We headed for the parking lot.
I assumed that his "ride" was the rust-colored, hardrid-
den Hippie-icon Volkswagen Beetle parked along the
curb. He quickly pointed away from the VW and toward
a shiny hot-rod, fire engine red 1970 Ford Torino Cobra,
complete with wired hood latches.

Bernie's passion for liberal causes, in seeming con-
tradiction to his love of muscle cars always puzzled me.

Perhaps it was because his father had been in the car business, instilling in Bernie a love of power under the hood and beauty in the design. This car was beyond mainstream and totally opposite the world of a Volkswagen owner, or, in my mind, a student activist. It seemed to bring home the point that no life is easily categorized or predictable.

Bernie longed to follow his gift for teaching at the college level. Nothing in his background, however, would have prepared him for the contemplative life of an academic. His father loved to work a room of hundreds; Bernie preferred the quiet seminar, consisting of twelve serious students.

After earning his master's degree in English literature, he enrolled as a Ph.D. student at the University of Kentucky. How could he have known that a doctorate in English literature from the University of Kentucky in the mid-70s would lead to nowhere? Moreover, his selection of a specialty would prove to be a mixed blessing, mostly a blessing. Under the guidance of the gifted Dr. Robert "Bob" Hemenway, who was then the director of the University of Kentucky English Department and later chancellor of the University of Kansas, Bernie chose African-American literature as his specialty. Meeting and studying with Dr. Hemenway was an enriching experience. Bob had become a specialist in the genre of African-American literature known as "The Harlem Renaissance." The Harlem Renaissance peaked in the 1920s and was the coming out of the literary, musical, theatrical, and visual artistry of African-American culture.

While Bernie was still working on his doctorate, he and I moved to Florida. I had graduated from law school in 1979, and had taken a job with a small law firm in Lake Wales. He accepted a full-time teaching job at a small college and a part-time teaching job at another.

We soon realized that Florida was not for us. I was not happy with small-town life. Bernie was not fulfilled teaching at two colleges. A white man could not get a job teaching black literature anywhere. He followed me into law school after abandoning his quest to become a college professor.

Today, Bernie is a gifted lawyer, but that was never his true calling. He facilitates a book club consisting of young servers in the restaurants that we co-own with three others. He has introduced them and me to beautiful, unfortunately obscure, literature. Mirroring my life story, with no particular guidance into the world in which we found ourselves, he has thus found a way back to his calling through adaptation and creativity.

Their Eyes Were Watching God, a novel by Zora Neale Hurston, a famed writer out of the Harlem Renaissance and named one of the hundred most influential novels of the twentieth century[4] is one of Bernie's favorites. He buys multiple copies and, like an evangelist, never tires of handing them out to those longing for the extraordinary and inspirational story of Janie, an independent and spirited girl. Despite being poor and uneducated, Janie is independent and strong, as this passage from "Their Eyes Were Watching God" illustrates, "Janie saw her life like a

---

[4] www.thegreatestbooks.org

great tree in leaf with the things suffered, things engaged, things done and undone. Dawn and doom was in the branches." How prescient is that message to our life stories?

Mike Gobb

Hired as the executive director of the Blue Grass Airport in Lexington, Kentucky, in September 1998, Mike Gobb served in that capacity until January 2009. He joined the team with great fanfare. The Blue Grass Airport was founded, as many regional airports were, just after World War II, when communities began to awaken to the challenges and opportunities of a new global age.

Located on the outskirts of Lexington, Kentucky, next to the storied thoroughbred horseracing track, Keeneland—the airport and Lexington were poised to grow together, and Mike was the perfect hire. He was handsome, ambitious, and gifted. He seemed to know from the beginning how to take a small regional airport, located in a special place in the heart of horse country, to the next level.

Because I worked with cities, which were involved in nearly every aspect of public infrastructure, I would run into Mike frequently at transportation meetings. He seemed busy and always onto the next thing or event. I noted—even without knowing Mike well, that he was particularly unengaged in whatever business was at hand.

He would breeze into a meeting, work the room, and then be out the door. Handsome and self-confident, he had something neither Bernie nor I had—swagger. Swagger is a quality that can be friend or foe, and while it exudes confidence, it can cross over into arrogance and aggression. I thought he needed to show more interest in the matters at hand. At the same time, I envied his self-confidence that I never seemed to acquire.

I heard a rumor that he would buy cigars and distribute them to the states' congressional delegation to the members' great appreciation. I could not have imagined having such hutzpah. One observation of Mike after his death was, "We thought he was going to be governor someday." He seemed destined for even greater things than running the airport.

Born on December 10, 1962, in Wyandotte, Michigan, Mike developed an interest in the aviation industry from an early age. He graduated from Western Michigan University and started the life of moving up and onward that was common in the industry. You start out at a small airport, stay a respectable length of time, and then leave for a bigger assignment. That involved moving around the country. He doted on his beautiful wife and a daughter. For reasons to which we are not privy, his marriage ended just following his crucible.

Airports were Mike's entire career. He was airport manager at Alpena County Regional Airport in Alpena, Michigan; in executive management at Kent County Airport in Grand Rapids; and at Bradley International Airport in Hartford, Connecticut, before coming to the Blue Grass Airport in Lexington in 1998. He stayed there for a decade until the crucible that doomed his career and ultimately his life.

Mike seemed to love the adrenaline and excitement of running an airport. He enjoyed the risks that came with getting up each day, facing the same issues that might face a mayor of a good-sized city. It was heady work and many could not tolerate the challenges of wooing passengers in the highly competitive and changing world of air travel, along with the daily risks that require both a police and fire force on the ready. Airports often serve as the hub for job building within a community and economic-development professionals tout them as assets. They are frequently the epicenter of political intrigue. Unless gifted at tiptoeing through the minefield of issues, airport executives have a "short shelf life." It is one of the few professions where the next employer often overlooks an applicant being "fired." Decisions like additional runways that bring out the NIMBY (Not in My Backyard) crowd, noise issues, and lost airline gates can doom the CEO.

Mike had found his element. He hit the ground running in his coveted position as executive director of the Blue Grass Airport. He traveled extensively, visited with airlines, and successfully negotiated to secure gates at Blue Grass in the most competitive of times. He savored the competition of two airports: Louisville and Cincinnati—each just 90 minutes away. Mike was winning passengers and had received numerous accolades during his tenure.

Seemingly, without warning, it began to unravel. Though no one knows for sure, Mike says his addiction to pain medication began around 2003, with a simple trip to his general practitioner to seek treatment for back pain. The doctor, like many in those days, may not have been privy to the growing science of addiction.

I believe Mike's story. At the height of my career, former Governor Ernie Fletcher asked me to take a leave of absence from my "day" job and implement a strategy that he had in mind for attacking Kentucky's growing prescription drug-abuse problem. The drug problem was reaching its peak with the overprescribing of oxycodone. Once reserved for the most severe pain, it was being prescribed for minor pains. The "science" of pain medication has evolved, and now we understand the dangers of pain-medication prescriptions and the need for close monitoring.

I was reminded of the dangers of prescription painkillers when I shattered my femur in July 2010. During a visit two weeks following surgery, my surgeon asked if I was still taking pain medication. "Yes," I replied. "I do as the hospital doctors advised, 'two Percocets in the morning and two in the evening.'" He practically leaped across the room, telling me to stop taking the pills immediately.

"You take those long enough ... you'll be addicted," he admonished.

Implementing the Office for Drug Control Policy opened my eyes to the world of drug addiction. I visited rehabilitation centers and heard the heartbreaking stories of horrific and desperate acts undertaken for just "one more fix." The experience helped me to understand what had happened to Mike. The swirling vortex of intense coconuts rained down upon him. Because he was talented and high functioning, no one knew or guessed the worst. He had become an addict.

Mike's addiction played a key role in his ultimate fall from grace and in his death.

CHAPTER THREE

The Moving Finger

Writes

"The moving finger writes; and, having writ, moves on; nor all your piety nor wit shall lure it back to cancel half a line, Nor all your tears wash out a word of it."

—Rubaiyat, Omar Khayyam

August 2006: The Story before the Crucible

Walking my dog in the early morning of August 27, 2006, I smelled something burning. Bernie, who was then chair of the Blue Grass Regional Airport, came running up behind us. "I have to go quickly," he explained. "Mike Gobb just called—there's been a crash at the airport."

We would learn later that forty-nine lives were lost just minutes before, when Comair Flight 5191 fell from the sky. We live one mile from the airport, and the smell of burning jet fuel would hang in the air for days. Like a cloud of doom, it refused to dissipate.

Flight 5191 was on takeoff that day. Most who were lost were "locals" from Lexington and surrounding small, tight-knit communities. They were a cornucopia of beautiful people and of stories ending tragically—everyone knew, or knew someone who knew, nearly all of them. Mike and Bernie, being so involved in the community, knew most of them.

A young couple from nearby London, Kentucky, was embarking on a honeymoon; a young woman, newly engaged, was home for her first wedding shower and returning to work in Washington, D.C.; another was meeting her sister for a long-postponed cruise. Only the copilot survived. His injuries were so severe that he has been unable to remember what happened that fateful morning. The stories were indescribably painful and heartbreaking.

Bernie and Mike, along with first responders, arrived at the 5191 crash scene before anyone else did. It was a carnage of smoldering twisted metal, human remains and scattered wreckage. After the crash, I would often find Bernie chain-smoking in the darkness of night. I would ask, "What's wrong?"

"I can't get that scene, that awful smell, out of my mind," he answered. In the aftermath of the crash, Bernie was not alone in his suffering.

Mike was haunted by his own memories, more than anyone realized. Bernie shared that Mike was deeply troubled by the crash. Days after Mike's death, the *Lexington Herald*-Leader September 18, 2013, published an article, titled "Gobb's Service: Ex-airport Chief made valuable contributions," which offered glowing praise for his handling of airport affairs over the years.

He is quoted as saying about the accident, "You're so busy in the first few days and hours that you're not thinking about the emotional impact. ...It's when things wind down a little bit and you start to digest what you saw—that's when it hits."

The crash was just the beginning of the carnage and barrage of coconuts that would start to fly. This resulted in nearly unbearable stress on both Bernie and Mike. The lawsuits accused anyone and everyone. "Blame" coconuts were flying.

Bernie was the board chair for the airport at the time of the crash. He would take only one volunteer position at a time. That cost him opportunities to have a higher profile. He took on Little League during the time the boys played. He served as president of a neighborhood association, even having a tree planted next to the neighborhood recreation center in his honor for outstanding service. We laugh that most people get a "tree" when they die, but quickly note it is clear that being president of a neighborhood association is at least a "near" death experience.

The airport board as a whole consisted of a talented group of unpaid volunteer business and nonprofit leaders. The mayor of Lexington appointed them. These were plumb community leadership opportunities for service, and all knew they involved a significant time commitment. However, under the theory for most modern board appointments, the busiest individuals are typically the chosen ones.

Doing everything right, the board had established finance, audit, and ad hoc committees—the norm in the business. Engagement by board members was high. Overseeing an airport with 85 employees and all the typical issues endemic to the industry presented challenges— a stand-alone police and fire force; competition for passengers; and the operation of bars, gift shops, and restaurants, among others. Budgeting was a challenge, and revenue streams were complicated.

Airports across the country have a variety of governance structures. They are frequently referred to as "quasi-governmental" entities in keeping with their schizophrenic nature. Quasi, (neither fish nor fowl) as applied to such entities as airports, means that they may be regarded as governments or businesses. Such labeling can be critical when it comes to what is and what is not acceptable in expenditures and tolerance for other activities. However, the public did not elect the board members, and revenues were only tangentially tax dollars and, in some cases, were clearly not. Revenues consisted of privately negotiated fees with airlines and vendors.

What was permissible conduct by the board and staff with this particular airport and what duty of transparency it owed to the public would later become issues.

The 5191 crash turned the airport and those associated with it into the status of local rock stars. The public and the press were more than mildly interested in the crash, which included the issue of blame for the catastrophe. The questions and requests for open records later grew even more heated and voluminous, compared with other issues.

Open Records Requests (ORRs), commonly known as "sunshine laws," are of vital importance to democracy. They ensure the public's right to information that would otherwise remain a secret. Open Records law varies by state, though its role as the holy grail of democracy is solid. A sister set of laws concerns the opening of meetings, held by "governmental" entities, to the public and press. As social media and other information outlets increase in influence, more demands are made for transparency— people desire to know just about everything there is to know.

By necessity, Bernie became even more involved in his volunteer board chairperson's role. He increasingly fielded the inquiries and questions. Bernie was elected to an unprecedented third-year term, which he regrets to this day.

After the crash, people wanted and needed to know what had gone wrong. Bernie's volunteer job morphed into nearly a full-time job.

Lawsuits were filed; lawyers were hired and paid; and analysis conducted. The National Transportation Safety

Board finally concluded that the cause was pilot error.[5] A pilot's "human" error had led the airplane down a closed runway and past several redundant warnings. The airport was vindicated.

The community was left reeling in the aftermath of the crash. The airport became the focal point of the collective need to come to terms with an inexplicable tragedy.

The sheer number of memorial services was overwhelming. At the one-year anniversary, the community turned out 1,600 people strong for the memorial ceremony, demonstrating the importance of the airport as a symbol of unity. The tragic crash in some ways united the community in its common need to grieve and come to terms with what had happened.

Unknown to the board was Mike's growing addiction to pain medication that he had been prescribed around 2003, long before the crash of Flight 5191. It is unclear when Mike finally became addicted. The catastrophic airplane crash, which resulted in the deaths of so many and the legal carnage that followed, seemed to worsen Mike's dependency on drugs.

Looking back, Bernie recalled the numerous signs of Mike's addiction after the crash. Bernie's coconuts fluttered dangerously in the rising breeze, but still he did not

---

[5] *Lexington Herald Leader;* "Pilot error blamed in plane crash that killed 49"; Ortiz, Brandon, Patton, Janet, Ku Michelle; July 27, 2007.

"see" the storm coming. He observed Mike slurring his words during a presentation to visiting dignitaries. There were fumbled presentations and missed appointments. Rationalizations for his behaviors followed. Mike's employees, who were relied upon for reports regarding his well-being, always gave positive reports.

All this sprang from loyalty to Mike, but also out of a desire to avoid an unwelcome and inconvenient truth: Mike had a problem, a growing one, and that problem was swiftly becoming a problem for both Bernie and the board. There is a tendency to gravitate to the status quo and to deny that things are awry. Mike was exceptionally talented and able to provide a suitable cover-up that likely threw already busy board members off the trail. He was always on top of his game at board and committee meetings.

There came a tipping point when Bernie and the board were forced to come to grips with the realization that Mike was a "high-functioning addict." The board recognized Mike's talent and wanted him to return to his job as executive director, operating a world-class airport. They fronted the money for his treatment with an agreement that he would pay it back, which he did. Bernie and the board believed this to be an internal matter between them and Mike.

He left for treatment in July 2008. He returned around Labor Day in 2008 and, from all accounts, had achieved and sustained sobriety. However, the seeds of his destruction had been sown. In addition to the crash and discovery of Mike's addiction, the summer and fall of

2008 witnessed the world undergoing dramatic change
and stress. The recession was raging.

However, it was an exciting time for Lexington and
the entire state, having captured the prize of hosting the
World Equestrian Games (WEG), which are comparable
in the world of horses to the human Olympics. The event
was to be held in 2010, still two years away. With the recession in full swing, it was quite a coup to land the huge
games. Still, attendees were needed from every part of the
world, and attendance was slow in coming due to the
worldwide economic downturn. Everyone was doing everything possible to ensure that the games would be successful.

The "Great" recession was descending like a heavy
blanket, snuffing out the dreams and hopes of many. The
"many" were not necessarily the rich or the poor, who
are the usual victims of economic downturns. This recession affected your next-door neighbor, your friends, and
members of the once inviolable middle class. Bernie and
I lost more than one close friend to suicide directly tied
to financial ruin.

Fat-cat bankers were accused of making off with the
national treasury, sometimes in reality and sometimes
with "guilt by association." Media stories abounded of
CEOs shopping for million-dollar rugs and gilded toilet
seats. "Bailout" and "too big to fail" became catchwords
and phrases that served only to crystalize the growing
anger among those who were not too big to fail nor able
to be bailed out.

Traditional media outlets were struggling to survive. Even veteran news staffs found themselves fired or their benefits reduced. It was a Wild West of information overload. Bloggers or anyone with a mouse, a computer, and an opinion became an investigative reporter, spewing forth as judge, jury, and executioner, weighing in on every real or perceived transgression. They did so with anonymity and impunity. Anger and frustration ruled the day. The "drive-by media" of the day was searching for its pound of flesh. It was a horror show.

It was during the summer of 2008, in the midst of Mike's treatment at a rehabilitation facility, that reporters from the *Lexington Herald-Leader* began issuing ORRs to the airport about Mike and his airport-related travel. Work was under way on an article about the airport, with Mike and his travel expenses at the epicenter. The article, "A Sky-High Expense Account", was published November 23, 2008. It had been expected and presented with the usual template, providing lists of travel destinations both domestic and international, including the name of the conferences attended, along with a list of related expenses.

In the midst of the news blitzkrieg, Bernie became the spokesperson for the board, and the designated defender-of-the-airport policy and procedure, and of Mike. He did his best to explain the importance of travel (and the inevitable expenses). He justified the expenses by pointing out the importance to the city of acquiring new business, and praised Mike's past ability to bring new business and a high level of recognition to the airport.

Bernie met with reporters and editorial board members, emphasizing the upcoming World Equestrian Games and the international marketplace for attendees. He drew a distinction between the airport and a governmental entity. Unlike governments, which are monopolies in their communities, competitive airports must market and woo airlines and passengers for their dollars. After all, the Lexington Blue Grass Airport competed with airports in Louisville and Cincinnati.

What might have been a mere meteor shower quickly became a cataclysmic crash of planet-sized boulders. More revelations came. The story took on a life of its own, becoming the perfect storm of blame and backstory against a heated mayor's race, a failing economy, and dwindling trust in governmental leadership. People were angry; the world was crazy. While Mike's addiction was known, other more spectacular revelations were in the offing. Explanations for Mike's travel offered little comfort to those ordinary people who were losing their jobs, retirements, and houses. The story in the newspaper caught fire. What appeared more frivolous than travel to someone who has lost his or her job? It did not hurt that sensationalized stories sell more newspapers.

Although the story might have ended with more transparency and other changes in the airport's internal-control systems, it was not to be. The board had begun a due-diligence investigation of the airport's internal pro-

cesses. At a December 17, 2008 board meeting, an un-
named employee told Bernie a story of epic proportions.[6]

The employee told Bernie about a strip club visit by
Mike and his department directors while they were in
Dallas on a business trip in 2003. No doubt, Mike was at
that point addicted, or at least well on his way. The bill
(in excess of $4,000) was paid with an airport credit card.
It should not have been charged to the airport credit card
and the airport was not reimbursed.

Mike's story was that he and his fellow directors
were entertaining airline executives. Likely, the invoice—
as is typical—did not provide a clue that it was a strip
club. Bernie held a press conference to announce the deception. Mike had already resigned as the result of a
board ultimatum. Though news accounts differ, the incident occurred in 2003, when Bernie was newly appointed
to the board but was not the chairman. Contrary to some
media chatter, Bernie was not at the strip club, nor was
he the board member responsible for reviewing and ap-
proving expenses.

With the irresistible ingredients of sex and money,
the rest was predictable: gasoline poured onto an already
raging fire. Bernie's credibility quickly tanked, and the
firestorm grew. "Guilt by association" and "where there

---

[6] *Lexington Herald Leader;* "Airport paid tab at Texas strip club –
Credit cards canceled after $4500 visit comes to light";
Hewlett, Jennifer and Alessi Ryan, January 6, 2009.

is smoke, there is fire" became the battle cries of the press and politicians.

The local media focused more attention on the airport than on a perp-walk for a disgraced Wall Street banker. Articles and blog entries about the airport scandal were numerous. They melded together with the articles that came later about me, all containing a "drop-in" paragraph that would draw references to both disasters, Bernie's and mine. If you Google the phrase "airport scandal," you will see the volume of entries.

Bernie swears that the newspaper photographer took at least 50 shots in an apparent effort to obtain just the right one. The "right" one was often above the fold, in which he appeared slack-jawed and haggard. I tease him that he looks like he has had several slugs of moonshine. Bernie was a news headliner in the winter of 2009, as he ended his tenure as chair. The storm did not abate.

In 2008, Vice Mayor Gray requested that the state auditor perform a management audit of the airport finances. In a specially called board meeting, the auditor presented her findings. Bernie recalls that the auditor reported that the vast majority of airport expenditures were legitimate. After the report, a TV reporter approached Bernie and asked him how it "felt to be exonerated." However, two hours later, when the auditor presented the airport review to the city council, Bernie was shocked to hear that the language was ominous and accusatory toward the board. There was a cry from the city for blood, and Bernie's head was on the platter. Bernie, working to hold back the tidal wave, quickly lost clients and credibility. In early January 2009, the city council called for Bernie's resignation as chair and a halt to any future appointments to the board until the audit was complete. [7]

Bernie refused to resign as chair or board member. Some members of the council argued that the council did not have the legal authority to ask a chair to resign. That opinion won the day, and Bernie did not resign, but remained an additional week when his term as chair ended. He stayed on as a board member for almost two more years.

Bernie was to receive the prestigious 2009 May Day award from the local Fayette County Bar Association for overseeing the crash of Flight 5191. However, the group reneged on its plan. "Let's skip a year of giving the award," was the politically correct suggestion. He had become too hot to handle. This reveals one of the hidden gifts of the crucible. When you are in the midst of the battle, you can look to see who is still beside and behind you—those people are your true friends. Failure is a lonely place to inhabit.

Aftermath

Mike and three of his department directors faced a harsh reckoning. Mike had already resigned under pressure by the board. [8] He and the employees who were in Dallas with him faced criminal charges. They were con-

---

[7] *Lexington Herald Leader;* "Council Ask Chair to Step Down – Newberry Criticizes Preliminary Vote"; *Ku, Michelle,* January 7, 2009.

[8] *Lexington Herald Leader;* "Gobb steps down, Resignation immediate no severance new questions involve use of other's credit cards"; Hewlett, Jennifer, January 3, 2009.

victed (or plead guilty) of misdemeanors and felonies related to the strip-club scandal, and other real and perceived irregularities. [9]

Mike was convicted of two theft by deception felonies, and given a suspended sentence of five years, with probation and a requirement of community service.[10] To this day, Mike's firing and subsequent felony convictions, remain controversial. I have heard that the judge received letters on both sides of the argument: that Mike should spend the rest of his life in jail on one side, to a few who held the opposing opinion that he should not be punished at all.

We were told that Mike did not realize that he would be pressured out much less be a convicted felon. He still believed his career and perhaps marriage could survive the onslaught of the coconuts that would ultimately prove fatal to him, ending not only his career and marriage, but also ultimately, his life. Mike had not spoken to Bernie since the day of his resignation.

Though he deserved some level of punishment for his transgressions, was this over the top? Despite the tragic ending of his career, Mike continued to work hard on his recovery from addiction. He searched for a new position in central Kentucky and consulting work in his

---

[9] *Lexington Herald Leader*; "Ex-airport director Gobb pleads guilty — Admits to 2 counts of felony theft by deception in plea bargain"; Hewlett, Jennifer; June 19, 2010.

[10] *Lexington Herald Leader;* "Ex-airport chief gets probation sentence includes drug testing, community service—Judge cites substance abuse, lack of criminal record"; Hewlett, Jennifer, August 14, 2010.

beloved airport industry. That was to prove impossible because of a felony conviction.

It was after Mike's initial anger about having been fired that he and Bernie reconciled. Sometime in the fall of 2010, Bernie contacted him to see if he was okay. They then assumed the roles of Bernie—wiser and older—mentoring the younger, more broken Mike. Despite the substantial career and financial setbacks and notoriety in the press, Bernie displayed the same steadiness and leadership and counseling strengths that were an integral part of his nature.

Although Mike found little forgiveness from others, Alan Stein, a well-known local entrepreneur, gave him a chance in 2012. In an act of leadership and courage, Alan took Mike into his consulting business. Alan not only gave Mike a chance, but he made sure everyone knew about it. Though Bernie and Mike had reunited years earlier, Mike and I did not reconnect until I went to work for Alan, as well. Mike and I jokingly and lovingly observed that Alan specialized in taking in the stray dogs that no one else wanted.

Mike and I would talk about our unlikely fates frequently over coffee. I would urge him to use his gifts as a speaker to give back to others the lessons he had learned from his experience. However, Mike held high standards for himself. He was unable to find work in the aviation industry, which he loved, at a level at which he would have been satisfied. In fact, he could not find steady work of any kind. Repeatedly, he faced rejection that proved unbearable. I begged him to move away from central

Kentucky and embrace a more ordinary life, jokingly re-
ferring to opening a hardware store in Peoria. He had lost
his family and his dream job. He could not find his way.

On September 11, 2013, Mike committed suicide.
Mike loved Bernie and in his "last" letter found following
his death, he wrote:

> "If you are reading this, you already
> know that I have passed. I have strong faith
> and know that I am safely in God's hands,
> pain free and at peace. First, and probably
> most importantly, I would like to take this
> one last opportunity to thank you for all that
> you have done for me over the years. You
> stood by me through thick and thin. You are
> and always have been a true friend and con-
> fidant. Love you like a brother, Mike"

These were the words of extinguished hope and belief that tomorrow would be better. He wrote of his
charmed life and asked that we celebrate and not mourn.
He told Bernie, "I will see you in heaven." We hope and
believe that Mike found the peace that so eluded him at
the end of his life.

Because he turned to an overdose of pills, many believe that he never kicked his addiction after all. I disa-
gree. I am convinced that he did recover completely from
his addiction as far back as the fall of 2008, when he was
released from rehab and began another nightmare journey. In despair, at the end, he slipped backward and relied on his old friends, pills, to do the job.

During his probation for the felony convictions, Mike reported regularly to his probation officer and was subject to random drug testing. He was quite compliant. I even recall that when hospitalized in the summer of 2011 for a biopsy, he vigorously rejected pain medications, fearing that he would violate his probation. I heard that his probation officer attended his funeral.

In his final years, Mike embraced religion. He was well known in his apartment complex for spontaneous and gracious acts of kindness. Bernie, as Mike's friend and attorney, was responsible for wrapping up Mike's affairs. He stopped by the apartment complex to look after, and begin the process of removing, his belongings. He heard stories from distraught neighbors about how Mike delivered hamburgers and drinks to workers and was always first to offer a cheerful greeting. Those are often the stories of individuals who endure a crucible. They understand better through crisis how to live a better life, appreciating others more.

I frequently relive my own shortcomings in Mike's life. I sent him an e-mail on the weekend before his death, knowing that he had been distant and withdrawn. I wondered if he was "all right."

"I'm okay; not great, but okay," was his reply. How I wish I had driven to his apartment in a final effort to offer hope in the face of what must have appeared to be diminishing odds.

Mike was gifted, and his contributions to the world would have been immense, likely far beyond his contribution as a CEO. He simply could not get past his past. He was stuck in the crucible, reliving each painful moment. To get past our past, we must be able to envision a brighter tomorrow. For Mike, it was not to be.

Could Mike have overcome his demons if he had been better prepared for what happened? Could the board have made better decisions along the way? Could we better assist others in spotting impaired coworkers, managing their treatment in humane and helpful ways, instead of throwing away flawed people? Could Mike have done more to balance his extreme talent and ambition with a better work/life balance? Could the community have been more forgiving? Could we as individuals have been kinder? Certainly.

In his final posthumously delivered letters, Mike requested a memorial service that would be a celebration of his life. Mike asked only two people, Bernie and Alan Stein—the courageous entrepreneur and leader—to deliver eulogies.

While standing outside the church, composing himself in anticipation of eulogizing Mike, Bernie was approached by a woman he did not know. "Are you Bernie Lovely?" she inquired. Offering his hand in greeting, he soon realized this was no friendly encounter. "You should not even be allowed here after what you have done!" she exclaimed before stalking away.

Returning to the church, he was ashen-faced and trembling. Determined to deliver a message of hope and redemption, Bernie delivered a beautiful tribute:

"I remember the story of the giant sequoias, those massive and majestic trees whose grandeur awes and overwhelms all who behold. They are indeed a marvel of nature in that they, for all their size, are not deeply rooted trees. In fact, standing alone, even moderate winds would blow them over. They grow as a forest, their shallow roots intertwining with those of their neighbors. With this community of roots, they cannot be toppled, each tree contributing to the strength of the others. So, too, are we. When we realize and nurture the amazing grace with which we are endowed by our Creator—shallow though it may be compared to God's—when we are able to forgive and forget, and when we are able to befriend as Jesus did Michael, we give and receive the strength necessary to sustain our life and the lives of others. It is this Mike asked us to celebrate."

The "mystery woman," who had spoken so harshly to Bernie before the service, knew Bernie only as the man who demanded Mike's resignation. She did not see him as the leader who made choices in the swirling midst of a disaster. She symbolized the surreal atmosphere of those frenzied times. Bernie was blamed by some and praised by others for his performance during the crucible. Rhyme nor reason prevailed. Perhaps it proves the maxim that "you truly cannot please everyone."

As an addendum to the story of the mystery woman of the "you-can't-make-this-up" variety, Bernie was walking downtown a few weeks prior to publication of this memoir. A woman came rushing up. "I'm sorry, you don't know me and maybe don't remember me … but … I'm the woman who approached you in the church parking lot at Mike's memorial service. For three years, I have lived with that moment … I want to apologize to you for my outburst. It was just that I loved Mike so much. He was so hurt by what happened. Please accept my apology. Thank you … for all you did for him."

Bernie was, of courses, stunned. We both marvel at the strange nature of all that happened and the continued aftermath—both good and bad.

The Lesson

Develop within yourself the compass that points to the true North Star. It will help you navigate the darkest night.

CHAPTER FOUR

My Brilliant Career

"I love to see a young girl go out and grab the world by the lapels. You've got to go out and kick ass."

—**Maya Angelou**

"My Brilliant Career," a film set in Australia in 1897, is a story of independent-minded Sybylla Melvyn, who longs to be a writer. A rough-hewn teenager, her poor farming parents send her away from the Outback, to her wealthy maternal grandmother to find her a suitable husband. Rejecting the life of her rich relatives, she gravitates to her tribe—the servants. In the end, she returns to the outback and her roots to realize her dream as a writer. The last scene has her placing her manuscript in the mailbox with a look of deep satisfaction. I am drawn to this story—why? I find myself attracted to stories about those who understand who they are and stick to their core.

Throughout the trajectory of my life and career, I had boundless energy and good health. Being grounded was not my strong suit. I would take on just about anything that struck my fancy, likely sacrificing a healthier balance between work and family life. Perhaps I was avenging my parents' lack of opportunity and my good fortune to find so much of it.

My father was grounded. I recall overhearing a conversation between him at the age of 89 and my son David at age 22, who was experiencing that time in the early twenties, when dreams begin to downsize to the "art" of the possible. "David," my father said with emphasis, "things never work out."

I chuckled to myself as I concluded that this was ironically the statement of an optimist. My father had no expectations that his life would work out. All he had were unexpected gifts. He settled for the joy they brought him. So what if things did not work out—he still had his grand tales that consisted of traveling in the dismal bowels of the ship with all other conscripts to Okinawa, Japan, where he was stationed during World War II. In a cup half-full attitude, he thought not of the bleak part, but about how he got to see the world. Perhaps that is why he lived to age 92. He found peace and contentment within the context of who he was. I was by nature always unsettled with the status quo.

When Bernie and I returned from Florida in 1980, I searched for a position in the field of law—not actually practicing, but one in which I could be more involved in policy development, which reflected my love of learning. I enjoyed the stuffy classes of law school that many of my fellow law students abhorred or tolerated while waiting to graduate and get to real lawyering. I was just the opposite. I loved the educational part, but not practicing law. I had taken the Florida bar exam and turned around to take one in Kentucky.

Bar exams, given in every state, have different requirements for obtaining a license to practice. I have never forgotten the Florida bar exam and retain my place as a Florida attorney. I am also licensed in Kentucky.

The test was administered in a cavernous room in Tampa, Florida. Many of the 2,000 people tested in July 1979 were Cuban refugees. It was around that time that the Mariel Cuban boatlift sent an estimated 125,000 Cuban citizens to American shores, with the blessing of Fidel Castro, in the face of a Cuban economic downturn.

The woman next to me leaned over and whispered in my ear, "Most of them don't know English, much less American law." In her own way, she was trying to convince both of us that out of the limited percentage of the test takers who would pass, she and I were in the safety zone. Taking the bar exam doesn't exactly bring out the best in anyone. For the short time we were in Florida before returning to Kentucky, I did estate and tax work, as well as working on a handful of "orange" truck-accident cases. Think Central Kentucky and "horse" law, and you get the gist of "orange" truck-accident cases.

In January 1988, I was approached about the position of Director of Intergovernmental Affairs at the Kentucky League of Cities. One of the KLC staff members spotted me while I was representing citizens in a utility rate case on behalf of the Kentucky Office of the Attorney General, in which I served as an assistant attorney general.

My initial response was that I had no clue as to what a Director of Intergovernmental Services did. When told it was lobbying on behalf of cities in the state legislature, I answered "yes," despite being clueless about the duties of a lobbyist. My career continued to play out in its usual uninformed and untamed trajectory with my willingness to try just about anything.

KLC, founded in 1927, is a membership association with an average of 380 city members throughout Kentucky. Forty-nine sister organizations are located in every state except Hawaii. Think of the American Association of Retired Persons (AARP) or the National Rifle Association (NRA) to understand associations. The function of associations is bringing like-minded entities and people together to share services and most importantly to lobby for common initiatives, laws, and revenue sources.

Associations, by definition, can be described as self-interested. They work within their governance structure to serve members with training, communications strategies, and lobbying for their positions in state and federal statehouses. The NRA is the most obvious example of an association with a strong sense of self-interest and identity. With countless members, the organization holds to its strong Second-Amendment beliefs, leaving little room for debate. In answer to movements for banning or limiting guns, the NRA would reply that its job is staunchly representing the views of the members. It is the job of others, not of the NRA, to challenge its views.

KLC, while small in the beginning, grew over the years because of strategic choices and entrepreneurial programming. When I left the organization at the end of 2009, the annual budget had grown from a million dollars to more than $54 million and from 10 to 80 employees.

Lobbying satisfied my love of the stage and provided a seductive sense of power and of being part of big important policy decisions. It was a path away from the practice of law. I had been fired from a divorce case for being too nice to the "other side." I wanted a job where being "nice" was a virtue, and this was it.

I hit the ground running. My job was keeping city officials happy by helping pass legislation that would enable them protect the public through law enforcement, filling in the potholes, and recruiting jobs. Our sons were young, and Bernie was practicing with a private law firm by that time. Before my job as a lobbyist, I could not have told you who our governor was; afterward, I became a political junkie.

Becoming a lobbyist satisfied the itch that drew me to law school in the first place. I grew up viewing the old Perry Mason TV series, which aired from 1957 until 1966, long before Court TV and Judge Judy. Think of lobbying as a profession of persuasion—not very different from being a litigator in a courtroom and convincing a jury to your viewpoint.

Being nice, not only to legislators, but also to their staffs who serve as gatekeepers, is key to being a good lobbyist. I truly enjoyed the work and, more importantly, the people. A lobbyist's job is to pursue a cause. In a rite of passage, a lobbyist will from time to time be on the receiving end of a tongue-lashing by an angry legislator often staged in front of a crowd. It is a lobbyist's job to buck up, check ego at the door, and find a pathway to success for your cause. My job was scurrying around the feet of those in power and keeping my eye on the prize of winning some important piece of legislation or killing it. I was a natural.

Through well-practiced humility, my great staff and I were able to get key legislation enacted on behalf of cities. Those issues included such arcane and complicated matters as more taxing authority, a lower cost of borrowing money, and mandated police training, to name just a few. I was especially proud of getting a constitutional amendment enacted to allow a different borrowing method for local governments, which saved them money.

After joining KLC, I observed, while Ed, my predecessor, implemented programming that would transform the organization into one of the largest associations in the Commonwealth of Kentucky. Nationally, KLC came to belong in the same league with larger city organizations in states known for big and bold initiatives. Those included the North Carolina League of Municipalities, the California League of Cities, the Texas Municipal League, and a handful of others. Perhaps KLC had grown too big for its britches, as my mother would say. Perhaps its ambitions were too lofty. I had often heard that Kentucky "eats its seed corn" and abhors success. That offers one theory with regard to our lack of Kentucky's long-term job growth and economic success.

KLC-member cities ranged anywhere from "wide" places in the road to the cities of Lexington and Louisville. Most of the cities were small, fitting Kentucky's profile as a rural state. A board of directors, composed largely of mayors from throughout the state, governed KLC. Each year, a new mayor would serve as the volunteer president. He, and sometimes she, would serve as the chair, much like Bernie's position at the airport.

It had been clear to me for months that Ed was seeking another job and would be leaving KLC. Having built the organization to the precipice of success, he seemed ready to advance to another challenge and leave the next phase to someone else. He walked into my office one day, closed the door, and announced his impending-departure. To my surprise, he suggested that I apply for his position as CEO. With that invitation, he had over-looked longer tenured staff members and remarkably, approached me, a woman, for the opportunity. There were few women leading these organizations. Women were barely breaking the ranks of the lobbyist profession, much less that of CEO. I was humbled by his confidence in me.

Friends—whose advice I sought—immediately questioned my interest in taking the position, reminding me that my current position was a "dream job." I could work in peace at a role in which I was comfortable and proficient. I would not have the responsibilities of the CEO position, and my days would be structured and manageable.

My ambition and desire to move up to the next level were kicking into high gear. However, I had young children, and Bernie had a demanding job. When I mentioned that to Ed, he assured me that the organization was poised to plateau and that it required the stabilization I could bring, while furnishing the basic services that our members needed and desired. One mayor's resistance to my efforts to land the position troubled me. Charlotte held the distinction of being the first woman mayor in the state. She had taken that success story to another level by becoming involved in KLC as president one year, and other statewide leadership positions. She was in great demand for her superb leadership qualities and competence.

I considered Charlotte to be a mentor, and we frequently discussed the challenges that we faced in the tough environment of politics. Though we never discussed the issue, she and I were women leaders surrounded by men. Women had always been part of the lobbying profession, but not always in the role they desired. I have heard the tales of women lobbyist pioneers who were appreciated not for their analytical abilities, but rather for their homemade cookies or fried chicken.

"Schmoozing" was expected of lobbyists. This consisted of hanging out in the after-hours bar scene, hoping to catch a moment with someone important to a particular legislative cause. I was not a schmoozer; I can barely stay awake past ten o'clock at night, much less hang out in bars into the wee hours of the morning. In one of the only instances I was criticized by a board member, it was because I didn't "schmooze." I refused to bow to the pressure. There were lines that I would not cross, despite my ambitious nature.

When I finally decided to submit my resume for consideration as KLC's CEO, I contacted Charlotte for a reference. Upon telephoning her, my request was met with stony silence. Had I totally misread her earlier support? Growing increasingly uncomfortable with the silence, I was ready to hang up and reconsider such a bold step. I wanted Charlotte's approval.

Finally, she broke the silence. "I wish you wouldn't do it; it is so hard for women," was her solemn reply. As if she had breached some sacred code to not dampen ambition in younger women, she quickly followed with, "If this is what you want, then I am happy to recommend you."

Charlotte had seemed unhappy for the last year that we were together in the "halls" of power. In the lead-up to my request, we had seen little of each other. I had understood that she lived in a rented apartment in central Kentucky to accommodate statewide leadership positions that emanated out of Frankfort, the state capital. Her husband practiced dentistry in western Kentucky, three hours away.

With no knowledge of the details, I knew that she moved back to Western Kentucky. Did Charlotte weary of fighting a battle that neither she nor I could clearly identify or admit to? Did she "get it" long before I did?

I accepted the job and took it on with zeal. I was bound and determined to prove myself worthy of the trust that had been placed in me. I would improve the lives of cities and city officials. In addition, I was driven to have these people like me and approve of everything I did. I would work 24/7. Nothing was too large or too small, including crisscrossing the state at all hours to breathe life into my vision. I developed a huge contact field. I was deemed a visionary.

The Stories

I discovered the other side of KLC that I came to love. That side was getting to know some of the most wonderful and intriguing people on earth—local leaders. I relished hearing their stories. At the urging of one of the mayors, I began to record their stories on index cards. I marveled at the diversity of their backgrounds. It seemed that anyone could run for mayor—from a cemetery worker; to the polished Mayor Jerry Abramson of Louisville; to Charlie Beach, a bank owner and talented mayor of Beattyville, Kentucky, located in the heart of Appalachia. Though there were bad apples, most were united in a call to service for ensuring that others had a decent life.

I became mesmerized by politics. Even in small towns, elections are often brutal contests filled with accusations, one-upmanship, and promises no one can keep. I met leaders who knew how to do the right thing and did it, no matter the consequences.

Local officials were at the bottom of the totem pole of power. I leapt into high gear, providing leadership development, training sessions, and general hand-holding to enable our local leaders to thrive and do their jobs better. And, I collected their stories.

Mayor Charlie Honeycutt, instead of retiring, was elected mayor following a career as an award-winning band director in Glasgow. Recognized internationally, the band traveled frequently to competitions around the world. In one instance, on their way to a band contest in the southern United States, Mayor Honeycutt marched his biracial band out of a restaurant when refused service. He was ahead of his time.

And there was Mayor Paul Smith, my mentor and a former U.S. adjutant general. On a detour from a cushy retirement in Florida, he settled—temporarily, he thought, as he cared for his ailing mother—in his birthplace of Burkesville, Kentucky, a tiny town in southern Kentucky. The lifestyle could not have been more different from his high-flying, globe-trotting days as a general. He built the largest likely unsellable house in Burkesville overlooking the Cumberland River. After his mother died, he could not sell the house. He settled, ran for mayor of Burkesville, and was elected.

As a leader in my organization, Mayor Paul Smith brought military discipline and management expertise in

developing strong operating policies. Many of those policies and procedures came under fire during my crucible
for reasons I cannot fathom—except that they were
complicated, as fitting our complex organization. Perhaps
unwittingly, Mayor Smith's work added to the confusion.
He was long gone when the crucible arrived, and I
missed his wisdom.

Mayor Smith (never one to withhold his opinion)
and I met with the local newspaper editorial board one
day to discuss our dissatisfaction with the coverage of a
particular issue. We believed the reporter had inaccurately
portrayed the facts and hoped to set the record straight.

The editorial board members responded with non-
chalance. According to the mayor, who wouldn't give up,
"We, at our organization, will always admit when we are
wrong and apologize." I winced, knowing the futility of
his efforts.

"You know that the newspaper makes mistakes, and
yet you never apologize," the mayor boldly told the editorial board. "And, in the meantime, careers and reputations are ruined." They ignored him and, looking at their
watches, quickly left the room on their way to the next
"important" meeting. He was a staunch conservative and
not a media fan. On the other hand, I was liberal and a
strong supporter of the media, even when I thought they
got it wrong. In fact, I remain so today. Mayor Smith and
I were, in many ways, a mismatched pair—he all Fox
News, and me all CNN.

There was humor in the stories. Commissioner Robert Coleman of Paducah was lamenting a robbery at the local Walmart. Walmart and other big-box stores were feverishly building stores across Kentucky and other small towns throughout America. Downtowns were being gutted in a transformation that carries on even today, while many that were once thriving retail centers struggle to survive. Commissioner Coleman observed with a sigh of resignation and frustration, "I guess everyone ends up at Walmart…even thieves."

My zeal for the stories of these unsung heroes led to writing two books: *The Little Red Book of Everyday Heroes*, about some of the heroes I had met along the way, and *The Little Blue Book of Big Ideas: New Cities in America*, about how visionaries around the world were building great cities.

The *Little Red Book of Everyday Heroes* features Mayor Brad Collins of Morehead, Kentucky, a small town in the heart of Appalachia and home to Morehead State. The story of Mayor Collins was inspirational and made me thankful for having come to know him. He grew up in substandard housing in a poor family. He became mayor so he could make a difference, particularly in ensuring that adequate housing was provided to all. Shy in public, but emphatic in his vision and service, he told me, "No child should ever endure such bad conditions. There is nothing more important, nothing nobler that you can do, than to provide a family with a safe, decent, affordable home." Despite poor health, he continued his work and courageously broke ties on city council votes that he personally and religiously opposed, but felt were important for the long-term economic strength of the city. He did the right thing over and over.

My files are filled with stories of dedicated public servants. In my opinion, the 90s were the golden age of local public service. No doubt, my deep engagement in the lives of so many color my opinions. The really good ones were connected by a strong sense that, when fortunate in our own lives, we owe back to others.

In addition to growing our lucrative insurance and financial-service programming, I continued the progressive trajectory for KLC. Loving media and communications, I revamped an older publication into the award-winning City. I made speeches throughout the country and founded the NewCities Institute, a separate 501(c)(3), with a goal of seeking support and funding for innovative projects. I published two books, was profiled in positive articles, received numerous awards, and was known throughout the country for my vision and expertise. It was heady.

I was touted for political office. I was successful ... until I wasn't. When I fell, I fell hard and with a thud that ricocheted through my life, work, and relationships. It would be a bullet that damaged not just me, but those most precious to me—my family and friends.

CHAPTER FIVE

Bonnie and Clyde

"It's the proper time to fly into hell."

—Arthur Miller, author of the play "The Crucible"

The winter of 2009 continued to be steeped in the airport revelations. Mike and his managers were under investigation, and pursuit of justice was in full swing. After January, Bernie was left reeling from his experience in the political circus.

In the early winter of 2009, KLC received its first ORR from the *Lexington Herald*. It was the same newspaper that was investigating and writing sensational news stories about airport irregularities, both real and perceived. Some of my board members and staff were stunned to receive the request, but not me. I had already assembled the pieces of the airport story and how it would lead to me.

But, even given my strong belief in transparency and the public's "right to know," I felt that the requests were overly intrusive. KLC, as far as the board, staff, and sister organizations across the country believed, was a private association business. Why would we be subject to ORRs, which are aimed at public entities supported by tax dollars?

By its very definition, an association business is not subject to ORRs or to Open Meetings Laws. Like all associations, KLC focused on issues germane to those members, and privacy was a major tenet. As an association, we were expected to entertain, sponsor receptions for state leaders, set our salaries, and otherwise develop a work plan around boosting our members' well-being as dictated by our governance structure.

But, KLC was complicated. The city of Lexington was among its 380 members, which led to its designation as a "governmental entity" by those seeking information. The argument by the newspaper was that the 380 KLC members were cities. Therefore, KLC was a governmental entity supported by tax dollars and thus subject to the Open Records Laws.

KLC was and is an "association business" that represented 380 city governments, which are supported largely by taxpayer dollars. It was a quasi-governmental entity, capable of being defined by interpretation. Dangerous. Given this login, even private entities are subject to full disclosure as all serve the public.

Through the efforts of my predecessor and continued by me, significant outside streams of revenue were being generated to supplement membership dues. The absurdly low $300 annual dues from the smallest city came nowhere near supporting a staff of 80 and the broad array of services offered. Like similar association businesses, KLC had aggressively developed "non-dues sources" of revenues. They included fees from insurance and financial-service programs, partnership fees with private companies that sought advertising in KLC publications, and sponsorships from interested vendors. All this represented a common association-business model.

In full agreement with my board, my initial stance was fighting what we believed to be an intrusion into private-association territory. Our argument was that the vast majority of our $54 million budget consisted of private dollars. A small single-digit percent of the budget reflected membership dues from cities. We maintained that we were private. The newspapers contended that we were not.

Under continued pressure, the board capitulated and submitted to the avalanche of ORRs that began in the winter of 2009, peaked in the summer, and gradually abated by 2010. I strongly questioned KLC's submission. As a lawyer, however, I could argue both sides. Once we gave in, we should have been consistent in our response. But we were not.

"What do we have to hide?" some board members inquired. What one person believes to be nothing can mean everything to another individual. My sense of foreboding grew with each request. This would not end well.

Because KLC was considered a government entity, any expenditure would rightfully be subjected to high-level scrutiny. I knew that we would not pass the test. What I didn't anticipate was how I personally would be cast as the villain. My board and I sustained a close relationship, and we were in lockstep about issues regarding expenditures. I suppose every story needs a villain and, as CEO, I was the logical choice. The coconuts began to tremble. This time you could see them shaking.

Intensity grew. I became the focal point of what seemed to be daily media inquiries. Like the November 2008 article regarding Mike Gobb's travel and expenses, "my" article was coming. I am convinced that this was prompted in part because of the Lovely and Lovely connection. What could be more enticing than a Bonnie and Clyde narrative? The first article to bear the fruit of the numerous ORRs appeared June 7, 2009, and it was all I dreaded it would be.

The Expense Article

My travel schedule, stays in hotels, my nice car and salary, and everything else became public information. It was Mike Gobb's November 2008 article all over again with only the name, dates, and places changed. The bloggers were on fire. One blogger even noted, "That picture of her must have been 15 years old." She was right. I had aged many years during that time period. It was quite a fall from grace: I had once been the darling of the press—no more.

I was being fitted for the scarlet letter of a pariah. A letter to the *Lexington Herald* editorial editor was "accidentally" published. It mentioned, among other things, that I should be "drawn and quartered for stealing public funds." The editorial staff issued me a private apology for the letter that should not have been published, according to the newspaper's own policies. "It slipped through the cracks on a particularly busy day," was the explanation.

What had been a bout of despondency in the spring of 2009 blossomed over the summer of 2009 into full-blown depression, for which Dr. Matheny—my dear friend and doctor—prescribed antidepressants. What else could he do when I sat sobbing during routine appointments? I was the epicenter of the storm. The articles kept coming. The media calls were incessant. I wavered between rage and catatonic trances. I recall sitting on my mother's grave, crying, and begging her for guidance through what appeared to be an unending torrent of coconuts.

On advice from my doctor, I visited a psychiatrist who, after hearing my story, assured me that I was sane and that she could not really offer any help. I just had to "live through it." I found comfort in the fact that I was assured of my sanity.

I still believed, in spite of the negative articles, that my career was salvageable. After all, I thought, I had received praise for my performance for more than 25 years.

Surely, I would rally and regain my footing. The coconuts came flying not one by one, but in meteoric showers.

Ironically, I had received criticism throughout the years from my board members because I tended to overwhelm them with paperwork and explanation. I documented anything and everything. They said I relied too heavily on them for decisions. I interpreted that as "weakness" and adjusted too far in the other direction. I went from over-documentation to moderate documentation. I made a huge tactical error in not keeping detailed notes. One lawyer, advising us on corporate structure, told me not to keep detailed notes because they could be misinterpreted and come back to bite me. He was wrong. I had difficulty documenting the decisions that the board had made. I, too, like the coconuts, had become unmoored. I was Alice falling through the looking glass.

I kept hoping for the news that would knock me off the front page, but my story seemed to trump everything. Was I that important? Unrest was global; unspeakable atrocities were being perpetrated; and local needs for housing and quality education abounded. Michael Jackson died June 25, 2009, and it seemed I was bigger news. One legislator told me that I got worse publicity than an ax murderer.

What had been a sleepy organization tucked neatly into the corner of importance was suddenly the center of attention and the subject of rage. My salary and others came under fire, even though they were set through a formal salary study. Which hotels I stayed in and the number of conferences I attended came under scrutiny;

an education trip to Romania to explore learning opportunities for mayors was the subject of intrigue.

During one "interview," I was asked, "Whose frequent-flyer miles did your son David use when he accompanied you on this trip?" He leaned forward in his chair as if to be ready to snatch me if I tried to run. I sputtered, like one accused of plotting the murder of a head of state, "I think he used his own." It turns out that he did use his own.

I felt like the accused who confesses to a murder she did not commit only to get relief from the torture. Ironically, I had at one time, years before, offered to donate my own frequent-flyer miles to KLC, just as I had successfully donated about $20,000 in fees that I earned speaking throughout the country. The offer of the frequent-flyer miles was refused; KLC did accept my $20,000.

My car was a favorite topic. It was a nice car. My board dictated its selection with what could be interpreted as sexist commentary: "That little woman should not be out on the highway late at night in anything but a nice, safe car." Mayor Smith, who drove a Lexus, was particularly exacting on requiring a high bar when it came to automobiles.

He knew of my travels throughout the state, giving speeches and visiting cities. He recognized how driven I was to make a difference in the lives of our members. Moreover, he realized that I wanted always to be home in my own bed anytime I could. It was not uncommon for me to be on the road at three a.m. on a dark interstate, traveling from far Western Kentucky, trying to get home after a dinner speech to a local chamber or Rotary gathering.

There was my visit to New York City to meet with an artist/benefactor in her nineties who was donating $100,000 to the NewCities Foundation, no portion of which was ever given to me. Her goal, and mine, was to raise the bar of art in Kentucky cities by placing her paintings in city halls to dress up often-drab places. This was all part of my plan to raise recognition of cities— how better than to make them art-friendly?

The June 7, 2009 *Lexington Herald Leader* article made it appear that I was in New York picking out paintings for my office. The implication was that I was lying on a chaise lounge with young, nubile men feeding me grapes. It was any- thing but that. I was there during a crippling snowstorm.

It was an onslaught of flying coconuts. I could barely look up to see my way through the storm. But, even larger coconuts were to come. July 2009 brought the worst. The board members grew defiant when asked for what they considered proprietary information about our insurance programs. The insurance division was their pride and joy and a lucrative, innovative, and effective business. The insurance company was enormously successful. Unlike other insurance companies, KLC knew the issues facing cities, particularly the dangers inherent in law enforcement, and worked hard to avoid both monetary and human losses.

The data sought by the newspaper would reveal that Bernie's law firm had a slight edge compared with other firms on providing defense work for KLC's insurance programs. The firm had many lawyers who worked on lawsuits and the story—as most stories are—is complicated.

Bernie had been with a small law firm that merged with a larger one, which was also on the "approved" list for providing representation, thus doubling their representation.

Bernie was well known among the mayors. They frequently asked for him by name. According to the mayors, his defense of their cases was particularly effective. Bernie loved the work, and the mayors loved him. One talent that both Bernie and I possessed grew out of our "salt of the earth" upbringings. We related well to gritty, "tell-it-like-it-is" small-town mayors.

All law firms, including Bernie's, were approved by the board and worked at the same hourly fee of about one-third of their standard rates. Staff assigned cases in the insurance division. The staff regularly evaluated performance, and Bernie's firm always got stellar reviews—not only for winning cases, but for cost-effectiveness.

Because of the perceived "conflict of interest," some thought Bernie's firm was not qualified. That had been discussed. We thought that by making every firm meet certain measurable criteria, we had taken sufficient care. In today's world of increased transparency and scrutiny, conflict of interest rules are evolving. Most allow participation by those connected to staff or board members when chosen in a clearly defined competitive process with full disclosure. We thought we had met the standard.

The board took a stand, despite the fact that it had already capitulated to the previous ORRs. That decision resulted in multiple disasters. On the afternoon the board deliberated about whether to release the information, Bernie told the newspaper editors that the information "would soon be released," based on my assurances.

As the airport story went from explosive to simmer, Bernie had developed a good, but fragile, relationship with the newspaper. To his and my surprise, the board reneged on providing the ORR. Bernie had to deliver the bad news, crippling the already fragile relationship. He was livid, and I recall this as one of the few moments when he and I sensed that the entire affair was driving a wedge between us.

After scathing articles appeared across the state about how I was stonewalling the press because "I had something to hide," the board agreed to the release of the data. It was too late. The damage was done. The state auditor announced that she would be performing an audit because there were too many issues arising from the dust of a quickly crumbling structure.

The state auditor's work began in the fall and concluded in December 2009, in a press conference, at which time a scathing report was turned over to the state attorney general for further investigation. As far as I know, that investigation never happened. Years later, I am puzzled because I know my staff and I had not committed a criminal act.

Career-Ending Moment

I had yet to endure August 19, 2009, and the ending of my beloved career. The board had had too much. It was time to cut out the cancer who, in this case, happened to be the once golden girl, the apple of their eye— me. I should have seen it coming. My depression continued. My nerves frayed by the constant media bombardment.

Trying to act as if nothing had happened, the KLC board and I soldiered on as best we could. My board's executive committee and I were attending a conference in Louisville dedicated to educating local officials. It had been a joyful time in years past, but not this year. Tension hung heavy in the air.

Two weeks prior to the conference, the board members stopped returning my calls. I heard that Mayor Newberry, who was embroiled in a mayoral election battle with Vice Mayor Gray, was making calls enlisting support for my ouster. Did he need a scapegoat because he had served on the board that was being accused of neglecting its duties?

My deputy—who had always claimed to have my back—was unusually distant, and I believe was likely working with a board member on my ouster. Put in charge after my departure, he sought the permanent position, which he did not get. This man had once been a trusted colleague and friend. The rats were fleeing a sinking ship and looking to drown the troublemaker. The cold shoulder was unbelievable. My head was spinning, and I was spiraling down. I was as if the little girl I once saw separated from her parents at the Atlanta airport. She had jumped on the tram and they, along with a younger child, did not make it. The doors closed, and the train pulled out. I will never forget the shrieks and the look of terror on the little girl's face as she was "abandoned." I could feel her pain.

I called a meeting of the KLC executive committee as instructed. This did not tip me off because we always had business to conduct and frequently held meetings at conferences where we were already gathered. I passed two *Lexington Herald-Leader* reporters just outside the hotel meeting room. The music was finally playing a recognizable tune. Was my story so important that it was worth deploying the precious resources of a newspaper down on its luck? Perhaps I should have been flattered; I was anything but. Something was up. I was Bambi prancing into a National Rifle Association board meeting.

As the meeting began, I attempted eye contact with board members, many of whom had become good friends. Most averted their eyes and looked down at nonexistent paperwork they likely wished was there. They were tired, and so was I. We collectively wanted to get back to the business of running a great and successful organization. After several awkward moments, I was asked to leave, along with the handful of staff members. The board went into executive session. Clarity finally arrived—I knew what was coming and braced myself.

I looked to my good kind friend and incoming board chair as I left the room. His eyes conveyed a message,

"There is nothing I can do." He was no match for those who wanted me gone. The bench outside the meeting room was my respite for what seemed an eternity. I tried small talk with my staff, but it was awkward, and we finally gave up trying. One by one, they went away. How has it come to this? I began to cry. Freda Meriwether—my longtime assistant and my dearest friend even today—held my hand and whispered assurances that all would be okay, one way or the other. Freda is one of those who catch on early. She had known for some time what was going down. I refused to read the signals.

Summoned back to the boardroom, the news was delivered; I was to "retire...or else." The room was charged with tension. A heavy blanket of doom hung in the air. It snuffed out any good will or support that I had. It was clear that the meeting had been contentious. Some board members had accused others of not "owning up to their own contributions to policies that proved our undoing." In the end, I was the collateral damage. I agreed to retire at the end of 2009.

I once again began to sob. In my usual fashion of seeking to turn any negative into a positive—and having convinced myself that all this was my fault—I circled the room, hugging each board member and thanking them for the opportunity to have held the job of a lifetime.

It still had not occurred to me that I could have a voice in all this, and being nice was not always the solution. Nevertheless, I was a "good girl" and went out without a fight. After the sobs and hugs, I rushed out of the room, refusing to talk to reporters. In one article written after my ouster my tears were the center of attention.

"Shortly after the league's executive board went into closed session, Executive Director Sylvia Lovely came out in tears but would not discuss what happened."[11]

I marvel at that. At first ashamed, I have regained my footing. Was crying a critical part of the story? Because I am a woman? Was it a sign of weakness? I did cry and do so even today when I consider my loss and how it could have been better been handled or avoided altogether. Today, I unabashedly confess to crying at sad movies, happy movies, and everything in-between. So does Bernie. I was weak at the time, which led to my mishandling of the whole incident. None of this fit the profile of the hard-driving CEO that I wanted to be.

The fall of 2009 brought a temporary respite from my trials and tribulations. With more flexibility, I was able to travel to Wisconsin to see my son and his family. I enjoyed some of the most beautiful fall weather that I can recall. I stayed in a hotel room in town and drank coffee in trendy Madison coffee shops in complete anonymity. There were no more ORRs, emergency board meetings, wringing of hands, and cries of "what do we do this time?"

I told Dr. Matheny that I wanted to stop taking my antidepressants—against his advice. I would go it alone. This was likely risky. My world as I had known it had col-

---

[11] *Lexington Herald Leader*, "League of Cities tightens ethics—New rules include it's first-ever conflict-of-interest guidelines" Blackford, Linda, August 20, 2009.

lapsed. I no longer received phone calls from those seeking my advice and counsel. It was clear that I had become a nonperson banished from the world in which I had found such joy and passion. Someone had died—me. Because I could no longer pull any strings, I was of no use to most of my contact list. That would get worse for a time. I spent a lot of time in contemplation and waiting for what I knew was the other shoe to drop—the issuance of the state auditor's report. I would receive periodic reports from Freda and others about the voluminous requests from that office.

Out of Africa, a 1985 film is about author Isak Dinesen and her love affair with Denys Finch Hatton. She is the hard working, "never give up" sort, and Finch Hatton is portrayed as a free spirit. A mutual friend warns Dinesen that, "Finch Hatton brings you gifts but never at Christmas." Their mutual admiration sprang from their differences. Observing her resolve to overcome all setbacks that came with a woman trying to make a life in colonial Africa, Finch Hatton observes her trait "to never stop trying." Like Dinesen, I continued to try. I did not have to come to my office any longer, though I would retain my title as CEO and my salary until the end of the year. Once again, I should have known. This message could have been more directly delivered with "don't come to the office again."

I had been elected chair of a group sponsored by the National League of Cities, consisting of those in positions like mine across the country. I was the only woman ever elected by my peers.

I held the office until the end of 2009. It was awkward, but I was determined to see it through.

Not absorbing the underlying message to "stay away," I continued to return to the office for special events. One painful event was the annual Halloween costume party, which I had pioneered years earlier as a time of celebration for the staff. My talented staff always came through with innovative costumes. We paraded through the streets and awarded prizes to the best. I had received the prestigious prize one year as a rooster. A pair of large "long" underwear, two pillows providing the oversized rear end, a comb and beak transformed me. I was hilarious. I never tired of making people laugh. It was the stage and I loved it.

I showed up at the Halloween celebration in October 2009, following my unofficial ouster. I spent a lot of time on just the right costume. I have since buried its description, along with an attempt to kill the memory of that painful event. I was not greeted with the love I expected. No one laughed as I walked in and began performing my "act." There was only stony silence, with my discomfort growing as I frantically considered a graceful exit strategy. The staff had clearly decided I was a liability and wanted nothing to do with me. Like those on my contact list, they saw me as no longer useful. I was finished. Freda, still employed at KLC, mercifully came to my rescue.

She literally pulled the plug on the boom box I had brought along and flashed me a look that said, "I love you. Leave; you are humiliating yourself." I said a quick "Good-bye" and I never returned. Their reaction broke my heart; but I understood. They had mortgages to pay and children to feed. It was time to admit defeat and start a new life.

During the fall months prior to my officially leaving KLC, two encounters stand out. While making a rare appearance at the office before my Halloween fiasco, I ran into a board member in the hallway. He had been a supporter and had become a good friend over the years, or so I thought.

We approached each other in our first encounter since my ouster on August 19; I wondered what to say for the few seconds before he passed me in the hall. To break the spell and fill the awkward silence, I asked, "How are things in the city?" He stopped and stared at me for several seconds, which felt like an eternity, before responding with, "And ... I thought you were bulletproof." I was speechless. He continued walking down the hall. As he passed me, I realized he was walking away from me—in life. I have not heard from him since.

In the fall of 2009, I had lunch with a longtime friend, a doctor and professor, who shared my love of policy. Together we had written an opinion piece sharing our support of progressive issues. It, along with my other opinion pieces and NPR commentaries, published over the years, were well received. He and I had planned more collaborations. He had observed my descent into deep depression and was desperate to jolt me out of it. When I arrived, a cohort of other friends whom he had invited to cheer me up surprised me.

As I approached the table, I began to weep from joy. One friend, in a reassuring gesture, put her arms around me and whispered, "It is okay; it will be all right … after all, we've never seen a woman stumble and get back up." I was shocked at her comment. Was my stumble that visible? Right on the spot, I decided to embrace her comment. I can tell the stories of woman who have stumbled and gotten back up. They can become the heroes we need to know. I can be one of them.

I left the luncheon with the bravado of a game-show contestant who wins the Hawaiian vacation on the first spin. My spinning had only begun. My journey to recovery was to have yet another setback and would be arduous and twisted. Not only did I stumble, but also each time I tried to get back up, I would trip again over the furniture in the dark room in which I found myself. I was tripping over my left foot and had yet to find my way out of the nightmare.

The final and nearly fatal blow to my recovery occurred in December, with the state auditor's announcement of the KLC management audit. After a relatively tranquil fall, I was in Washington visiting some of my old contacts and trying to gain a foothold on what I believed would be a consulting career, based on expertise developed over 25 years. I anticipated that I could turn things around and hit the ground running in 2010. I was wrong.

My Washington contacts were ashen-faced as one by one; I kept my appointments with as good a game face as I could muster. They, too, had heard the news, if not the entire press conference that was playing out back home. The visits were perfunctory, and nothing came of any of them. My consulting career was dead on arrival. I thought the coconut storm had ended in December of 2009. However, the straight-line winds had toppled more than my career; they had wiped out my future consulting career as well. After this, I was bleeding at the side of the road.

The fallout in the winter and spring following the auditor's scathing report was overwhelming. Some who had been supportive after my firing suddenly disappeared from my life. For some, the newspaper could be overlooked, but with the trusted reputation held by the state auditor, I was "proven" a bad person.

Newspapers, politicians, bloggers, and the public at large had scrutinized nearly every judgment I made as CEO. No one is capable of perfect judgment in every instance. As one friend put it, "Similar things have happened to me, just not with the intense public scrutiny that you endured."

Soren Kierkegaard, philosopher and author of *Fear and Trembling*, once said: "Life can only be understood backwards; but it must be lived forwards. In living my life forward, I have taken the time to look backward, to examine and to understand. My past has taught me some invaluable lessons.

Lessons Learned:

- Provide leadership when and where it is needed. I had stuck my head in the sands of depression and had allowed the coconuts to bring me down.
- Be prepared and confident in answers to questions about KLC's operations.
- Speak up. It is better to go out with a bang than with a whimper.
- Place trust more carefully; I needed to under- stand the Old Russian proverb: Trust, but verify.
- Know and accept that board members and management staff are not family nor even friends; I was angry with them. I needed to look in the mirror of self-realization.
- Understand that true love is different from "business" love. I discovered that I did not know those who surrounded me. If I had, I would have accepted that I was not their highest calling.
- Be more confident in my core and know that I did not need their validation to thrive.
- Learn to say "no" when necessary; I was adaptable to a fault, likely due to a lack of confidence. Like a chameleon, I could be anything I needed to be to get the prize I sought. Adaptability is a gift, but not at the expense of knowing your core and drawing lines in the sand.

- Develop a more balanced schedule. I should have abandoned my quest to be loved by everyone. I should have refused such assignments as the one that Governor Fletcher handed to me for starting his drug-policy office, when it was clear it would put my life into overdrive.

- Anticipate and prepare in advance for the ferocity of the coconuts.

In the end, however, we cannot always hold ourselves responsible for recognizing, ahead of time, every coconut that may come our way. Sometimes, you are the victim of a direct hit that you never anticipated and even with the foresight of a psychic could not have seen coming. You have to allow for acceptance and recovery. Moving-on is an under-rated skill. Moving-on and continuing your life story, however it twists and turns, are key. My board and I could have done many things better.

Lessons Learned

- Defined who we were more clearly. I had enlisted attorneys and accountants who assured us that our governance structures were sound. Did we consider all our stakeholders, though, and reassess from time to time, who they were and how important it was to be cognizant of their need to understand who we were?

- Understood our relative power to that of others.

- Understood the arena in which we played.

Politics is a blood sport.

- Been clear within the organization about who we were.
- Realized earlier that I worked for local elected officials and that my vision of taking their cities to a higher level was not their interest. They served at the basic level. Keeping potholes filled and enough salt on hand for the winter.
- Stayed in control rather than giving up control to others.
- Been more decisive.

Following the decision to capitulate to the ORR, we needed to stick with our decision. We fumbled and stumbled. At every juncture, we would question our decision. One of the strongest elements of leadership is "stick-to-it-iveness." Observe key inputs; analyze them; make decisions; and go with it.

In the end, I accept responsibility because I was the hired hand. Taking all the steps I have outlined might not have worked, but it would have left me with more confidence and perhaps avoided the unfortunate loss of dignity for me and for the organization. Had I recognized the signs of an impending storm, and understood its ramifications, I could have better shielded my organization. I would have made a stand—for me, my board, my staff, and, most of all, my family.

I know that what happened to me, Mike, and Bernie was a bizarre confluence of events and forces that marked the times. The cauldron was filled with a strange and toxic mix. The perfect recipe of a recession, and circumstances fed the raging fire. Outrage and anger on the part of all of us, including the media and the public, were understandable. It was political theater at its best.

Bernie and the airport board members were volunteers, giving of their time and expertise without pay or recognition. I was a well paid CEO and thus fair game. The others were volunteers, and Mike suffered from addiction. What happened to them was unconscionable.

A small vindication came with the IRS audit. The audit, according to the agent, was triggered "because you were in the news with so many alleged irregularities." Among the "irregularities" dispelled were the mileage logs that I had meticulously maintained as required to note my personal/professional use of the company car.

I had been able to document my activities. The IRS agent (in a telephone conversation when I was hospitalized with my femur break) observed that I was the most unfairly maligned person he had ever known. "Why didn't you fight back?" He asked.

"Because," I replied, "I am a good-girl." He issued a substantial refund check.

As I battled these coconuts, I was to find that there were more on the way.

CHAPTER SIX

My Year of Forced Contemplation

"It is in this loneliness that the deepest activities begin. It is here that you discover act without motion, labor that is profound repose, vision in obscurity, and, beyond all desire, a fulfillment whose limits extend to infinity."

—Thomas Merton

July 29, 2010

I was in my mudroom, feeding Dylan, an eleven-year-old German shepherd; Phoenix, a three-month-old German shepherd; and Boogie, a twelve-year-old blind Pug. I had named the puppy Phoenix for a reason. He was symbolic of my new start—a phoenix of mythological symbolism. He and I would together rise out of the ashes.

As I turned to put down the food bowls, I felt a pain like nothing I had ever experienced. Though I never fell to the floor, I heard and felt something snap. I quickly gripped the countertop and looked down to see my left leg dangling like that of a marionette, whose string had loosened. I had no muscle control, and my foot was flapping at the end of my leg, limp and useless.

My leg seemed detached from my torso. I did not know it at the time, but my femur had shattered. The countertop became my lifeline as time stopped. I carefully removed one hand from a death grip to reach for my cellphone, which was luckily just inches away. I called Bernie.

Bernie always stayed late at Azur, the restaurant that we co-owned with three others. I always left early; in restaurant parlance, I was "early-out." It is a business where—now—owners must stay connected, if not on site, at all hours.

"Come home—there has been an accident," I said calmly. He misread my calm demeanor and decided to stay a while longer at the restaurant, thinking it was nothing serious. No doubt, he took a few minutes to chat with customers as he made his way out the door. At one time, before my upheaval, I had been the gregarious one. Bernie had assumed that post as I entered the dark room of my reputation disaster.

Calm did take over in the face of disaster—not uncommon among accident victims. While tumbling down the street following a car accident, one survivor worried more about wrinkling his jacket than he did about his potential severe injury or imminent death. Perhaps the mind cannot quite grasp the truth in those moments.

And so it was with me. With the countertop serving as my anchor, I had also grabbed onto something inside me. If I were to survive, I had to behave rationally and work my way through this. I called once more: "Bernie, can you come home? I've had an accident," I explained in a preternaturally sanguine tone as sweat began pouring from my brow.

A few moments later, my son called from Wisconsin to share a joke. I laughed, and suggested that he might call back later, again calmly. That conversation has become part of the family lore.

When Bernie came home, he quickly grasped my dire circumstances. Still clinging to the countertop, I was sweating profusely. As he attempted to carry me to the car, I shrieked in pain. Neither of us had ever needed an ambulance and rarely a doctor. This was new territory. He began to sweat, and his voice was shaking as I overheard him calling 911.

Noting that I did not fall, the EMTs commented that they could not recall loading anyone on a stretcher standing upright. Every tiny move brought excruciating pain, which even Fentanyl could not snuff. I let anyone and everyone know that with shrieks.

The only thing that would jar me out of my calm was that indescribable pain. Suffering in silence was not an option. (Perhaps I had learned a thing to two about "not keeping quiet.")

And so, I began another chapter in my crucible. I call it my year of "forced contemplation" in only a way that reliance on a wheelchair, a walker, a cane, and kind and loving caregivers can bring.

***

Arriving at the ER, I had emergency surgery. In my drug-and shock-induced stupor, I began spinning tales. One was a request for transport by station wagon the next morning for an award ceremony honoring my past service as KLC executive director. It was a gathering of my colleagues from across the country in Annapolis, Maryland. I was determined to be there. That request was ludicrous, of course.

I was delirious and do not recall many of the tales I apparently spun. Even my underwear came into play. As I lay on the stretcher in the emergency room, I threatened violence if the removal of my panties involved contact with my left leg. I agreed to let them be removed with scissors, leaving my leg untouched. This was not an easy decision in the moment of my stupor. The panties had history.

In the summer of 2008, Bernie and I had gone to New York City to meet with a NewCities Foundation benefactor and to conduct other business. My luggage went missing, which I later found out was a common occurrence at big city airports.

Because Bernie and I were to meet the benefactor and her husband that evening for dinner, I needed appropriate clothes. I had packed nice things, including the nicest piece of jewelry I owned and had received from Bernie for Valentine's Day—black pearls. Because Bernie's luggage was not stolen, I believe the pearls were the enticement as the thieves rifled through bag after bag looking for goodies.

With no clothes except the informal ones on my back, a hasty Sunday afternoon visit to Saks in downtown Manhattan was necessary. Being an old-fashioned department store, it would have everything I needed. Starting at the top floor, Bernie and I worked our way down, beginning with a business suit that would double the next morning for a bond closing, which had also been scheduled during the trip. Next stop? Shoes. Easy so far. Finally, we arrived at the underwear department.

Quickly realizing that the cheapest pair of panties, bikini ones at that, cost $42, I began to fret about the cost. Only when Bernie threatened to walk out if I did not buy the damn things and get the hell out of there, did I buy them. Forty-two dollars is a hefty sum for a pair of bikini panties. Even in my fentanyl-induced, emergency-room state, I reluctantly agreed—rather than endure the pain of their removal in the usual way. I continued to spin the tale of the lost luggage, no doubt providing embellishment as I went along. I cannot remember any of that.

I do remember looking up into the eyes of a very kind-looking man and seeing his giant hand reaching toward mine. Oh my, I thought. There he was, standing over me as I lay on the gurney in the ER—Thomas Merton, the famous monk. It was a soothing face, a reassuring one that seemed to say without words, I will take care of you; do not worry.

This was significant. Thomas Merton, a famous Trappist monk and a resident of the Abbey of Gethsemane, Kentucky, is the author of 70 books. He has been an inspiration to many, including me, for years. His books include the famed *Seven Story Mountain*, written in 1948, named one of the top hundred non-fiction books of the last century. He was a poet, social activist, and one of my favorite inspirational writers. I found his words and perspective comforting as I faced my own recovery from the reputation disaster. Now, here he was.

Have I died, and he is ushering me into heaven? I asked myself. That was a pleasant thought. Reality soon returned. He was not Thomas Merton, monk, but Dr. David Burandt, an orthopedic surgeon called in on a Friday night to put Humpty Dumpty back together again. He was reaching out his hand to shake mine in introduction. He then announced that his intention was not to provide for my spiritual well-being, but to perform surgery first thing the next morning. I want to believe that he said, "God bless you" as he left. He was and is an inspiration.

I was moved to my hospital room with enough pain medication to relieve me of noticing just about anything. However, then there was the "blood" woman who always visited me in the middle of the night, or at least I think so. She had snow-white hair and shared with me how she enjoyed her nocturnal duties. I wonder even today if she was real—perhaps a friendly vampire?

Following surgery that took far longer than antici-pated, Dr. Burandt visited for a post-surgery follow-up. He was too serious for my comfort. I asked him, "Will I ever be normal again?"

"We'll have to wait a year to know." It had been a tricky surgery, lasting far longer than expected. "But, I hit a home run in putting your leg back together," he added. I thought to myself, I love an arrogant surgeon. My left leg is laced with metal from hip to knee.

He shared that he saw breaks this severe in much older people. I had been taking a bone-building drug for many years before my femur spontaneously shattered. Some studies of the drug I was prescribed revealed that it had a rare side effect, which weakened bones and result-ed in jaw and femur collapse in some cases.

I had half-jokingly shared with others that I was des-tined to be in the one-percent club by hitting the "jack-pot" on rare side effects. After all, I was coming off the rarified experience of being the target of a full-on media blitz. As disasters go, my fall was not a ten-story fall; it was as if I dropped from the Empire State Building.

While pondering my latest mishap, I noted that my family did not have any history of bone weakness, except for my 93-year-old grandmother with osteoporosis, which was normal at that age. I have been remarkably healthy with no chemotherapy. I was active before the break, and power walking was my specialty. The drug I was prescribed was routinely given to women in the beginnings of osteoporosis.

After my femur break, I joined a national support group of similarly stricken people, mostly women. I marveled at how athletic all of them had once been. The femur withstands the worst of walking and running, it is particularly vulnerable when in a weakened state. The doctors tell me my bones are permanently weakened, despite extreme measures to strengthen them.

After spending a week in the hospital and another in a rehabilitation unit, what had happened to me became clearer. Unlike during the reputation disaster, sympathy poured out from my newest tribe of friends. Most of them were in the restaurant and food business, to which I had gravitated following my "retirement." In spite of that, the constant rejections caused by my reputation disaster continued to haunt me as I tried even in convalescence to find work. I was not the retirement type and longed to be of use to the world.

As I grew physically stronger, my spirit weakened. Multiple rejections were coming at me as if it had taken six months after the disastrous auditor's report for the appropriate official "you are no longer welcomes" to wend their way through the system. I fielded a steady stream of letters and announcements that yet another board, on which I had served, no longer had a use for my services. Some were sympathetic, while others were brutal.

I had served on the board of a startup nonprofit for finding ways to deliver medical information to a lay audience. Because I represented local leaders, my participation was natural. Just as I returned home from the hospital, I received a letter from the chairman, who announced that I was no longer welcome on his board because of what he read in the newspaper. The tears welled up and spilled over. I was heartbroken. It happened repeatedly, with other boards.

The hurt and accumulated fear, pain, and suffering came through in my racking sobs. Was it ever going to end? I asked the cosmic question to no one in particular. The universe was silent....

As a way to make sense of my situation and mandatory confinement, I began keeping a daily journal solely about this medical experience. When I read it now, I recognize that it chronicles my frustration, helplessness, and anger.

My challenges were twofold: literally surviving a serious life-threatening injury and rehabilitating my reputation. I heard that one-third of women die within a year of sustaining a break as severe as mine. While in a rehabilitation hospital, I overheard nurses talking about a patient—an older woman—who had been released and had fallen again, re-breaking her hip. I caught a glimpse of her as she sat forlornly in a wheelchair, waiting for a room assignment.

"She is disoriented," said Nurse Kristen, who became my good friend and who was escorting me back from X-rays. "We know the ones who will return—they live alone." I never knew what became of that woman, but I made a resolution and a promise to myself to walk and regain my strength through exercise.

Exercise was always a big part of my life, but it now would become an even greater friend. I think of that woman as a symbol of so many of those who are hidden from the view of our medical system and from us. I wanted to assist her and others, but repeatedly found that no one wanted my help. It was as if I had died.

I began life post-operation in a wheelchair. I had to learn to live and move in new and different ways. The toughest part of that process for me was learning to, and needing to, depend on others—for just about everything.

Diary Entry: 8/11 - 8/14, 2010

I awaken to the alarm, having struggled with sleeping on my back with my feet elevated. I stay in bed until Bernie gets the dogs out. When the thundering herd has been fed and walked and all appears quiet "out there," I get up in a series of steps and swings and land my hands on my walker waiting by the bed. In slow methodical moves, I head to where Bernie had placed my wheel chair at the kitchen table. As I approach, I see his dear white-haired head bent over the newspaper while he catches the few moments of peace he will have in his day before going to work.

Then comes the inevitable moment when circumstances force me to ask for help. 'I need my coffee and newspaper ... when you get a chance,' I say as apologetically as possible. He jumps up immediately and delivers. I soon creep across the room on my walker to the kitchen and do as much as I can to prepare my breakfast on my own. I scoot to and fro on the walker in slow motion and struggle to put food on the plate. I am exhausted from the effort, and I cannot figure out for the life of me how to carry the plate and operate a walker at the same time. Bernie again comes to my rescue.

Diary Entry: 8/28 - 8/29, 2010

I remember my first shower following the surgery. I dreaded it because it took so much longer than when I had a normal life. However, I needed it and looked forward to feeling thoroughly clean. Showers are intensely personal ... unless you invite someone in for reasons other than bathing.

There you are—buck naked and completely helpless. Bernie had to lift me onto the bench that we now kept in the shower. The worst moment of all, he had to come back and wash my left foot. At this point, I just did not stretch enough over the metal that had taken the place of my left thigh from hip to knee. In sickness and in health. I never imagined that that part of our marriage vows would become so key.

When you have experienced physical trauma, everything about you changes both spiritually and physically. In some cases, the pre-trauma "you" never returns. That can be good or bad. You can find a renewal of, and thankfulness for, life that you never had. Physically, you are changed and not often for the good. My skin felt leathery after the surgery and never completely returned to normal. One leg is shorter than the other—causing foot pain and interfering with exercise—but I do walk every day, and I cherish it. I have learned to slow down because I no longer have a choice. I take better notice of my surroundings on my slower, less frenetic walks … another benefit of what some might call a limitation.

During my recovery, I launched an all-out effort to develop less dependence on either Bernie or David, my son, who was home from a break in law school. I fashioned an apron with large pockets, which I strung across the handles of my walker. However, the real stroke of genius was enlisting my bra in the cause.

It made an excellent caddy for necessities, including (I am not kidding) a cup of coffee, a roll of toilet paper, and a house slipper converted to a chew toy for Phoenix. I took my bra to a completely new level of functionality. It is amazing how adaptable I was, but then I had a great deal of practice my entire life, didn't I? I look back at the Miss MSU Pageant as a perfect example of talent for adaptability.

On my first day alone, Bernie fenced Phoenix and me into my tiny home office. It was never meant to corral a full-sized human being; a wheelchair; other disability paraphernalia; and a growing, rambunctious German shepherd. It did make Phoenix less likely to dine on shoes and furniture, which had gained him the reputation of being the most destructive dog I had ever owned. The downside was that I could not do a lot on a whim, like go to the bathroom. Instead, I learned to "hold" it for long stretches.

I asked my dear friend, Chef Jeremy Ashby, the Azur Restaurant chef and a co-owner of our restaurants, to walk Phoenix. I would observe their youthful exuberance and lament the loss of mine. Jeremy was in his early thirties, and Phoenix was six months old. They frolicked in the glistening September sunshine outside my home office window. The fallen leaves made for even more fun. However, fall is the time when nature reminds us of our mortality in the midst of beauty.

I would ponder the profound nature of those autumn leaves until reality came knocking. I had to pee. Getting to the bathroom in time became a balancing act between my procrastinating and my journey down the long hallway to the toilet. You do not know how much being able to "hold it" means until you realize that a walk to the bathroom is an arduous task when mobility is challenged.

Even the simple act of peeing had become a multitasking event—holding it; practically crawling down the hallway with whatever apparatus upon which I was dependent at the time; pivoting around; and pulling down my pants. My total concentration was required. That left me fewer moments to feel sorry for myself, and so it was an unexpected blessing.

Like a scientist working on a cure for cancer, I gave long and deep thought to getting Phoenix into the yard on my own and not taking up Jeremy's precious time. For the life of me, I could not figure it out. I could not step into my yard without navigating at least one-step— something that proved impossible, particularly with a spirited puppy in tow.

I was forbidden to place any weight on my "bad" leg, and thus I gave up. There we were in our tiny universe, Phoenix and me, with the old dogs sound asleep in the bedroom. We were quite a pair. Anyway, who said I was abandoned? Phoenix found me fascinating.

Trapped in my infirmity, I depended upon the kindness of others. They delivered far more than I deserved. I found myself devouring any reading material that I could get my hands on and writing like a fiend. I wrote essays, some of which were published by my old nemesis, the *Lexington Herald-Leader*.

I was particularly drawn to portraits of leadership. My favorite stories were those overshadowed by the "bigger," more popular news of the day. I wrote one essay titled: "Tragic Turns in Life and Death Raise Questions on What Is Significant," published January 27, 2012, in the aftermath of the spectacular fall of Coach Joe Paterno. He was destroyed by miscues involving a sex scandal. Clearly, I was contemplating all that happened to me in this piece:

"I am reminded of a fellow who said the local food movement spoke to him because growing some of his own food, cooking it, and watching family and neighbors enjoy life wrapped around the fundamental act of eating was fulfilling. He employed a strange word to describe the new life he had chosen; his choice to live this lifestyle was one of 'insignificance.'"

I observe our obsession with celebrity, fame, and all things big. Coach Paterno was revered and loved one minute, and despised by many the next. Had he fundamentally changed during that transition? Likely not, but he paid a price for celebrity. My point is that life's greatest joys come not in celebrity or fame, but in what society considers "insignificant." I note that Paterno died shortly after his crucible.

Coming to terms with what can happen to the most revered among us is a lesson of life from which we can all learn. While what happened to Paterno was unbelievable, could he have handled his crucible better than he did? I pondered those cosmic questions and had lots of time on my hands to do so.

Diary Entry: 8/28 - 8/29, 2010

Then there is the obituary of the week in *The Economist*.[12] Dead at 88 is Bill Millin, the then 21-year-old who jumped off the landing

---

[12] www.economist.com/node/16885894; *The Economist*; Bill Millin, piper at the D-Day landings, dies on August 17th, aged 88; August 26, 2010.

ramp at Sword Beach, in Normandy, on June 6, 1944. He held no rifle but rather—bagpipes. He waded ashore playing the pipes amid the unthinkable carnage. As a judge had observed in 1746, 'a piper was a fighter like the rest, and his music was his weapon.' As the article observed, 'He remembered the sand shaking under his feet from mortar fire and the dead bodies roiling the surf, against his legs. For the rest of the day, whenever required, he played.' The Germans later said that they spared him out of pity for this madman. What a mark he left."

Today, I reflect on my feelings during those trying days. Intellectually, I concluded that we all serve in many ways, both small and large. As in the case of Bill Millin, we serve in inexplicably strange ways. Emotionally, I had a harder time with all that. Perhaps I needed to tamp down my wild ambitions to return to where I was and embrace what was an interesting and provocative turn in my life. I cannot change what happened. Better to make the most of it for the good of others and of me. As long as we have life, we have a chance to live a good life and do good works. I wanted to believe that, and I was determined to find my own bagpipes.

Diary Entry: 8/22, 2010

It is a busy Sunday, and my morning is filled with the newspaper and *The Econo-*

mist. [13]I love the short bios that *The Economist* publishes in each edition. This week it is about Robert Doyle, who died at 100 years of age. He graduated with a degree in architecture in the thirties, only to find that the Depression had ended his hopes of building grand buildings. By serendipity, he turned to the new "art" of art director in the nascent cinema industry of Hollywood. As films grew more sophisticated, he entered into a new kind of architecture, of sets for movies and scenes that provoked the feelings and emotions of the characters and the stories on the screen. He worked closely with Alfred Hitchcock, who was the master of the art of filmmaking. I had forgotten about Hitchcock. To remember him ages me.

I devoured these stories of comebacks. They were often about opportunities that came after defeats—some of them by chance and others by determination. There was hope for me to find something useful to do and leave a legacy of good works, however tiny. That is all any of us should desire.

Despite my physical limitations, my obligations did not stop during my year of forced contemplation. My father, at the age of 89, needed attention. My mother had been dead for many years at that point. His eyesight was

---

[13] *The Economist*, Robert Francis Boyle, art director for Alfred Hitchcock, dies on August 1st, age 100; August 19, 2010.

failing due to macular degeneration, and his hearing loss—no doubt from the noise on the factory floor—grew dire.

The workers had safety glasses and earmuffs, but did not don them until word was passed that the inspectors were on their way. He described the rat-a-tat of the drill presses where he worked and regretted not taking better care of himself, which is a common reflection in old age. He could no longer read his beloved newspaper and, though I longed to read it to him, he could not have heard me had I tried.

My mother died December 19, 2001, and thankfully did not live to see the devastation to my career. I do not say that lightly. She was very proud and, unfortunately, lived vicariously through my accomplishments. She kept every article written about me, which—until the time of her death—was all positive and celebratory. I also found out that so did Big Bernie, Bernie's father. We found a large file folder filled with articles about me after his death. I was the embodiment of their hopes and dreams. I was sad that I had let them down.

I was determined to protect my father from news of the reputation disaster, but he would surely find out about my leg and my long recovery.

I wanted to understand what had happened to me. It was always on my mind. In particular, I would recall such moments of incredible spiritual pain such as the dreaded call to my brother, Keith—who lived with my father—on the eve of the publication of the first negative article in

June 2009. I put the call off for days and finally, on the night before the article was to appear, I called Keith.

I asked him to take the newspaper off the stoop the next morning and hide it from Daddy. "Why?" he asked. "It is very negative ... about me," I began haltingly. "It will say that I did bad things." Silent for a moment, he inquired, "What do you mean ... did things? I do not understand." It was unfathomable. I was the star in the family, and overnight I had become an embarrassment.

He began to sob. Finally, he regained his composure and, in a strong and firm voice, he promised, "I will get those newspapers up every day; you can count on me, Sis." It was then that I began to cry with him. I love my brother and my family. My heart ached for what I had done to them. I was humbled by his steadiness and loyalty.

When the articles began to come in waves, my brother repeatedly and dutifully took up the newspaper. He later shared with me that Daddy would call the Herald Leader each time the newspaper was a "no-show," demanding a credit on his bill. I could hide newspapers, but I had no choice but to tell Daddy about my medical disaster. How else would I explain my absence from his life for a long stretch of time? David gave him the news.

"So, she can't drive?" he asked David. "Papaw, she can't even walk, much less drive."

When I lost my job, I lost my company car. I remember the day I was cleared to drive following the accident. In a moment either of insight or of pure coincidence, Daddy handed me the keys to his 2006 stick shift

Chevy S-10 pickup truck and announced in an act of pure goodness and, on his part, leadership: "Sibya (my nickname), I don't need to drive anymore."

My brother and I had contemplated the moment when we would have to take his keys because of his failing eyesight. He spared us by recognizing his limitations on his own. Knowing when to quit shows strength of character. I look back on that car with love.

My father's pickup trucks were symbolic of something he needed in his life. It was about being a man in the world in which he grew up.

He had sacrificed and gone without material possessions for most of his life so that my brother and I could do better. The gift of the truck was profoundly moving, and my eyes welled with tears at the grand and selfless gesture. The truck had none of the amenities that graced the modern executive car that had been mine. It was a Rolls Royce to me. I loved it.

Then there was the clutch. Regaining my strength, I finally mastered the art of employing it with my left "metal" leg. With a cup-as-half-full attitude, I concluded that pushing in the clutch was just the exercise I needed. I found that stretching to reach it was an added benefit because the bench seat was never going to accommodate reaching anything on the floorboard with my 5-foot-2-inch frame. I adjusted a fluffy pillow at my back to assist me in my endeavor to drive safely. On one of my first outings, I drove the truck to Madison, Wisconsin, again to visit my son who was working on his graduate degree in chemistry.

Terror struck just outside Indianapolis, when the engine light came on. Once again, I began to sob. I called Bernie, who suggested I turn around and come home. With determination, I kept going, and eventually the engine light went out and never came back on during the entire trip. Fortunately, I made it through Chicago and its twists and turns, and the obstacle course that was construction in progress.

Why did that truck suddenly straighten out? Perhaps grace was visiting in that moment. None of us understands the plans of the universe—how a little white 2006 truck might figure into the grand scheme. The truck was "passed-on" to our son David and served his needs until it literally died on the highway one day. Just as surely as losing a loved one, I mourned for the loss of that truck. It was an important part of my story.

As the truck became mine, I was responsible for taking my father on outings. One of the first post-surgery trips was to Meijer's, one of the ubiquitous big- box stores. He loved the place for reasons that remain puzzling to me. My parents grew up in the rough, but beautiful hills of eastern Kentucky. All their lives they grew gardens, cured their own meat, and knew every tree and flower that bloomed.

Perhaps he loved Meijer's because it offered him what he never had as a child—a veritable treasure trove of colorful things that could be possessed or at least touched and stroked, as in my mother's case. When she was dying from the ravages of cancer in late December, we would spend hours in Walmart with me by her side.

She would lean on a cart and troll the aisles, stroking the pretty velvet little-girl dresses.

Diary Entry: 8/20, 2010

I drive his truck over to get him. We park in the outer lot, next to a cart corral to make him exercise by getting a cart.

Slowly, we make it to the entrance. I am slower than he is at this point. I joke that I beat an 89-year-old to that milestone. Me on a walker and he leaning on a cart, we must have been quite a sight. Bernie said the newspaper would have loved a photo. I cringe at the thought of 'making the news' again for any reason.

We head past the produce to the 'cafeteria.' In a time-honored ritual, we stop at the cake department, where he orders two coffees. He pays and, while at it, fishes out five dollars and gives it to me for gas in the truck. I call it my allowance. We sit, and I wait for him to say something amazing and then scramble for paper and pen. Inevitably, he delivers.

A table of what appears to be Meijer's managers is sitting near us. My father suddenly turns, and we inch our way toward a faraway table at the end of the cavernous undecorated and colorless room. A few workers appear to be having lunch.

"Why don't you sit near our usual place?" I ask Daddy.

"When I see bosses, I always head faraway for the back tables."

"Why ... you are as good as they are. You can sit anywhere you want."

As if insulted that I challenged the world, as he knew and accepted it, he replied, "I don't fit in with them":

That was it. He was not to be engaged in class warfare from an upstart daughter.

I was learning more every day about my physical vulnerability and dependence on others. A sense of mortality, humility, fear, anger, and even humor all mixed in a year of confinement in a tiny room with a German shepherd puppy. It was a cauldron of confusion, frustration, and an overdose of self-absorption.

I grappled with everything, ranging from "where did I go wrong?" to "was I merely a cog in the machinery?" It brought home the realization of my tiny part in the grand scheme of things. What made me such an easy target? Weakness? Perhaps. As in war, Bernie, Mike, and I were collateral damage. Like the poor, illiterate young men in Harlan, Kentucky—who, Bernie observed, were nearly forced to pass intellectual and physical tests to be drafted during the Vietnam War—we were on the front lines, and we were cannon fodder. Media and politicians needed a win, and we were fish in a barrel. Not realizing my vulnerability early on was my greatest failing throughout my crucible. I assumed my own importance, but only in the eyes of others. I failed to grasp the reality of my weaknesses and to develop the core that would allow me to survive the direct hit of a coconut.

Diary Entry: 8/21, 2010

Had an adventure last night. Went to dog-training school with Phoenix. Poor Bernie. Once we finally found the farm, he had to get me out of the car and keep a spirited dog leashed at the same time. I had to be lifted into my wheelchair, and pushed up a country road, onto gravel, and finally down a steep hillside. The chair tipped at one point, and I began to sob. Bernie had it all under control, I know ... but it was frightening. This, on top of the humor of dog school. Nine dogs in all varieties, with owners as proud as they would be at the first day of kindergarten for a child. It is amazing how much people do look like their dogs. The comic relief was welcome.

It is another day, with nothing outside my little office. Actually, I have to say that I am experiencing something so strange and new. For the past year, I have been free-falling through angry clouds. All of a sudden, after a near-death experience, I've begun to float. The fear is that I do not know where I am going to land. That is perhaps my last frontier—that I will never know the Answer. I have to give in and accept. You cannot make this up. This moment of vulnerability and disability brings out my reclusive side. I sense that the turn is a good one. I send emails, but I care less about whether they go un-answered.

In many of my diary entries, I rail on in anger regarding what happened to me. Like assembling the famous Bush deck of cards on evil Iraqi leaders, I put together my top-five list and rearranged the deck from time to time. It would be a fantasy and a contest to whom I would send a nasty e-mail about what they had done. I did not send them.

Rather than recovering in a straight-line trajectory, I found myself slipping in and out of the depression I hoped to leave behind. I would relive the moments of humiliation—being deposed from boards, and losing speaking engagements and consulting gigs. That seesaw of reliving the horror and then sinking into more depression continued unabated.

Diary Entry: 8/28-8/29, 2010

I am feeling rejected and isolated, in spite of my efforts to fight off the demons. Should we ratchet down our expectations? Mine are high. I've given up on changing the world, but would like to make a contribution. Use my skills and talents. I fear ending up on the couch watching soap operas. I am pariah to those with whom I would naturally ally ... I came up with a name for a book— Knocked on My Ass at 60!

Not ANOTHER One?

I thought I had experienced the worst physical pain possible with the femur break until Friday night, September 17, 2010, nearly two months following the accident.

It had started out that morning with a metallic taste in my mouth and a shoulder ache. I disregarded the taste and decided that the shoulder ache was a pulled muscle. Before the femur disaster, I had never been sick in my life, and—according to my surgeon—I was mending quite well from the surgery. I had graduated to a walker/cane and used the wheelchair only for moments when I was especially tired. It never occurred to me that this was serious.

Sitting on my restaurant patio that Friday night—my pain was growing worse. A woman was pleasantly chatting, and sharing her day and plans for the weekend. I was barely paying attention because my pain was escalating. Even today, I feel embarrassed when I encounter her at the restaurant. I quickly excused myself and left for home. I tried lying down, but found it too painful. I wanted pain medication, but not since the initial days after the break did I have such a difficult time getting up. I sat on the couch, waiting for Bernie to return from the restaurant.

I clung with hope to the theory that I was experiencing a muscle pull. I was convinced that if Bernie would come home and bring me pain medication, all would be fine. As Bernie walked in from the restaurant, I requested two Percocets. He responded, "We are going to the hospital." At this point, he was good at spotting danger. This was no ordinary pain. This was no muscle pull.

Arriving at the ER in a car and not an ambulance did not lessen my dread of having another medical emergency. I am a healthy person. *This cannot be happening.* After numerous tests, as well as the definitive CAT scan, the doctor said I was experiencing a pulmonary embolism. Life threatening, it is akin to a heart attack. "You are lucky you made it to the hospital," the doctor told me. The clot, which began its journey at the site of my surgery, lodged in my lung, on its way to my heart. If it reached its destination, I would die. It was that simple. Having since researched the symptoms, I found that it was all there, just like a heart attack: severe pain in my chest and back, and shortness of breath. Only the metallic taste remains a mystery.

I remember being asked if I had shortness of breath. Though not being able to catch my breath was a very real symptom, I said "no." It was as if denial would translate into "this isn't happening to me, and I'm going home." To the contrary, I was immediately hospitalized, administered a heavy dose of blood thinners, and told not to move because that would cause the clot to move ever closer to my heart. I was terrified. For the next several days, it was "wait and see."

I spent a total of 18 days in the hospital, beginning with the July 29 break, followed by a rehab hospital, and now this.

Once again, Bernie played a heroic role. It turned out that Boogie, our aging pug, was sick and throwing up when Bernie arrived at the hospital to check on me the next morning. My instructions were simple, "Take him to the vet. You have too much on your mind to put up with a sick dog."

After Boogie came home and I was finally out of the hospital, I stopped by the vet's office sometime later to pay the bill. "Two thousand dollars," the receptionist said. It nearly put me in the hospital again. Today, I laugh at the memory. Remember, humor is a big part of acceptance and leadership. I will have to say that it was not funny then.

As I was leaving the hospital, the doctor told me that the clot was still present, but hopefully dissolving. "Watch for chest pains, excessive bleeding caused by the blood thinners you are now on, and shortness of breath. They are all signs that the clot is on the move and the threat imminent."

"You seem awfully serious, doctor." I was proud of myself for finding humor in the grimmest of times.

"Ma'am, you've had a pulmonary embolism." He pivoted and walked away. So much for humor—this was apparently no laughing matter.

I did find one "fun" doctor, who told me that from now on, I should avoid all knife-throwing contests and motorcycles, not necessarily in that order. I have adhered to that advice and have taken each of those off my bucket list.

While in the hospital for the second time with the pulmonary embolism, I joined several other patients in the hallway outside the X-ray department, waiting for snapshots of our broken bodies. Dr. Burandt would be evaluating my progress, not in his office, but this time in the hospital. I discovered that this was no ordinary gurney lineup. Like discovering the bagpiper on the beaches of Normandy, I was to find another extraordinary person who was about to change my life.

I was at my emotional bottom. I looked around and imagined that, given those dreadful open-back hospital gowns, we were in a kind of perverse booty call. All of us, including me, were broken individuals, most likely in spirit, as well as in our bones. The others looked so sick and old! Surely, I didn't look like that, or did I? The "gurney cop"—charged with the duty of moving us along—approached me, and we struck up a conversation. "Why are you here?" she inquired.

In a fit of self-pity, I poured out my story. She heard it all—the reputation disaster, the mysterious femur break, and the pulmonary embolism. As if signaling her need to tend to people with far greater needs than mine, she walked away with a life-altering statement: "I see here an opportunity for growth."

Her words hit me hard. I pondered how I had fallen into a pit of self-pity, but also noted the gift that I had been given. As if the clouds were clearing, with patches of sun, I was beginning to see that which I had not seen before. I was realizing that, paradoxically, it was not all about me. I was coming out of my insular world. I needed to love others and myself for what we are and appreciate all our contributions, small and large. Others had it far worse than I did, and suddenly, I saw gifted people in every walk of life.

Following my encounter with the gurney cop in the hallway, a man whose name I would never know returned me to my room. As I rose to get into my hospital bed, I realized that my gown was open in the back, revealing my unclothed backside. When I awkwardly began to grab for a cover-up, this kind man gently reached over, tied the strings of the gown together, and patted me on the shoulder.

It was a small—but significant—act of kindness, for which he received no praise, prize, or raise in his pay. There was a world of leadership outside my city officials, and there were gaps of assistance to the world that needed filling. Perhaps I could still contribute.

It was in that moment that I felt the beginnings of recovery. I experienced a greater sense of urgency to embrace my story and use it to help others. Could this be the true beginning of my recovery after fits and starts? Like the springtime that brings sun and flowers only to be blasted by a wintry storm, both my spiritual and physical trials were far from over. My recovery continues to this day.

Finally, out of the hospital and on blood thinners, the doctor asked me not to travel. Sitting stationary for any length of time can encourage more clots to form. Bernie and I had scheduled a tiny vacation to the Florida Panhandle, but we canceled.

I had managed to land a speaking gig in West Virginia, in October 2010, and a team of wild horses would not keep me away. By this time, I had graduated from a wheelchair to a walker. Ignoring my doctor's advice, I made elaborate plans to drive three and one-half hours to Charleston, West Virginia. I would stop frequently on the way and—in an elaborate ritual at various and sundry fast-food outlets, would maneuver my walker and make my way around the parking lot for stretching exercises. My reward was a cup of coffee.

I would be speaking from a Power-Point presentation I had put together. It was the rudimentary forerunner of *Dodging Coconuts.* The talk was well received by some, but not by others. Some felt sorry for me. I was puzzled by that reaction until I realized that not only did I talk about being hit by metaphorically flying coconuts—I looked as if I had been battered by one.

During the fall of 2010, I began once again to attend board meetings for the Morehead State University Board of Regents. I had served as chairwoman and was in my second year in that role when the president and others on the board gently shared with me that though serving two more years were the norm and I was doing a great job, I would be better off stepping aside. Left unsaid was that they would be greatly relieved not to have the burden of my glaringly bright scarlet letter that could be seen from the moon. While I resisted at first, the handwriting was on the wall. I had lost their support, so I did what I had become accustomed to doing since my string of disasters —I acquiesced.

I was becoming more used to rejection and regaining my footing. More and more, the sun was peeking through the clouds. Just as I thought I was getting it together, something happened that propelled me through the looking glass. I had accepted the assignment of serving as the chair of the Kentucky Cervical Cancer Coalition, one of the final boards for which I was still welcomed.

At the urging of the dear and courageous Dr. Robert Hilgers, an OB-GYN physician, I agreed to serve because my mother had died of the disease in 2001. Dr. Hilgers founded the organization because he grew tired of "seeing too many women die of a preventable disease." I wrote a very personal account in January 2011 (Cervical Cancer Month) about my mother's struggle and death from the disease.

The objectives were putting a face on this terrible cancer and encouraging women to pursue the opportunities for early diagnosis. I approached a fellow MSU Board of Regents member, who is an outstanding retired journalist. I asked if he would run interference with the Louisville Courier-Journal to publish the op-ed.

At the next board meeting, I asked if he met with success in getting my article published. His long silence alerted me to his answer. He told me that his successor, the editorial board editor, had rejected the piece unless I could make it appear that someone else authored the article. THIS IS ABOUT MY MOTHER. Who else could write it?

"You should call him," was his response. I called, but received no answer. The op-ed was never published. My anger at the world grew.

Physically, I have my "ups and downs," but am determined to make the most of my compromised bone health. I am under the care of a bone-mineral specialist at the University of Kentucky. When I arrived at his doorstep, he used random numbers to describe my bone health. For a woman of my age, he observed that I should be at a level fifty. I was at a dismal five. Though I resisted, he prescribed a daily injectable, Forteo®— known to strengthen bones, but with a warning for bone cancer. The Food and Drug Administration limits lifetime Forteo usage to two years because of the cancer warning.

When I asked about the cancer risk, he replied in a thick German accent with descriptions of studies of rats on the drug that indicate the rare nature of the side effects. "But," I countered, "I am the one rat out of 400,000 to whom all this has happened."

When my two-year stint on Forteo was up in November 2013, my doctor announced to me that there was little more he could do. He is a dear man, who was genuinely saddened by his helplessness. No other drugs were in the pipeline to address my deteriorating bones. My bones had increased from a five to a thirty due to the therapy I had received, but the number fell short of the magical fifty. "But," he suddenly brightened up. "There is one thing. Some studies, though not scientific, have shown there is a machine that appears in some cases to build bone. The so-called jiggle machine vibrates your body as you stand on it and exercise."

I immediately researched the so-called power plate. I learned that the machine is increasingly appearing in chiropractic offices and exercise gyms. It is the successor to the better known "butt-jiggler" that was popular in earlier times with a belt across one's rear end, presumably lead-ing to weight loss.

I joke that because my birthday is in November, the same month in which I purchased a power plate, that Bernie bought me a giant vibrator for my birthday! Have I told you what a great husband he is?

Looking on the bright side, Phoenix and I have a new adventure. I descend into the basement of my home, where my beloved "jiggle" machine resides. Phoenix an-ticipates our visit with great pleasure. When we arrive at the machine, which is about my height with handles, I hold on and begin to squat and jiggle away as I stand on the power plate. For his part, Phoenix attacks the ma-chine—biting and barking at it with the fierceness of a frontline soldier eliminating a threat to his republic. If he could talk, I believe he would tell me that this is better than any squirrel, bird, or rabbit that dares to provoke him within the perimeter of our backyard.

I was ready to move on and gain a toehold on what was to be a new life, with lessons learned, emerging out of the darkness.

At age the age of 60, I was prepared to take the "les-sons learned" in a year of forced contemplation and move forward to study what had happened to me and produce teachable moments.

Among those teachable moments:
- I have the gift of a story that is uniquely mine.
- I learned that many others have greater needs than mine. I should drop pitying my-

self.

- I perfected my gift of adaptation to be more consistent with who I am.
- I learned how each phase of life adds another chapter to the adventure.
- I discovered that we grow from those experiences.
- I learned that adversity is a gift, if you are willing to use it for "good."

I needed to learn that springtime matures with sufficient nurturing. Others could learn from my story and that of others who shared the stage with me. I was on to something.

The road to recovery is bumpy ... but worth it.

CHAPTER SEVEN

Humility, Hutzpah, and Humor

"Don't come back from hell empty handed."

—"Don't Come Home from Hell Empty Handed" by Barbara L. Mackoff

"You don't know what a burden it was until you lose your reputation" is a phrase attributed to Margaret Mitchell, author of *Gone with the Wind*. I recall hearing this for the first time in the midst of my crucible and thinking: what a great thought … if only I was gutsy enough to embrace it. I still have to believe that a reputation is something to be treasured. I suppose it all depends upon how reputation is defined beyond "the quality of your character as judged by people in general."

Though caring what others think of us is overrated, the fact is that it matters on a professional and personal level, so long as we wish to live among our fellows. We are creatures of community, and our "tribes" are important to us. By extension, the reputations of organizations with which we are a part suffer when those who work within them run headlong into the reputation buzzsaw. It can take years to recover, if at all.

If I could interview Mitchell about her words, I would ask, "What prompted you to say such a thing?" I have searched, but can find no answer. Let me speculate. She might say that she intended to be provocative to get attention to her point. I have shared this line in speeches, and the reaction is denial of the legitimacy of such a thought. Following the initial reaction, I detect more thoughtful, contemplative looks.

Mitchell would follow up with this: Losing a reputation is not a good thing, except for a certain freedom it offers. Reputation loss was what turned my life to a more positive course. I cannot change what happened, and would if I could, but perhaps I should take it as a signal to live a better, more creative, and fulfilling life.

I am like the successful young man in his mid-thirties who laughed with me about how, even if our fellows forget, Google never does. Because he knows that every prospective employer will likely Google him and unearth the DUI he received in his early twenties, he shares up front his journey from a DUI to becoming an even more responsible young man.

He and I both acknowledge that reputation loss is not the ideal way to learn how to grow up, but it can result in growth. Could it be that adversity, no matter its type or quality, is good for the soul? Have we discovered the salvation and a true value of Google?

We are what we are, and why hide our stories? The world is increasingly dangerous for reputations. Perceptions of wrongdoing, real or perceived, cannot be erased. We live with information bombardment and the threat to responsible journalism by entertainment news and blogs.

When I was young, police often drove a tipsy son home leaving him to parents ready to deliver punishment. Today, thankfully, we are getting drunks off the road any way we can. However, many young people do not know the consequences. They can be barred from certain jobs.

My reputation was perhaps too important to me and, when I lost it, I nearly lost my life. I had to find my way; I had to discover my stories.

After I navigated through my crucibles and spent a year in forced contemplation, I realized my stories had been dormant for too long. That is true of many of us. Amidst the hubbub of our lives, our unacknowledged stories brought to light can provide insights and guidance. Rarely have we reached even middle age without at least one crisis. What might happen if we tapped into crisis to learn and to help others?

Why should we care about our stories? What are we seeking, and why is our quest so compelling? The proliferation of self-help books and memoirs is informative. As the sixties anthem put it, "Somethin's happenin' here."

The world of today is not more barbaric than in the past, but our exposure to chaos and violence is more instantaneous and global. Opinions about anything from the funny to the serious are virally shared. We now can learn in seconds via the Internet what might have taken weeks, months, or years before. The information is sometimes presented to us out of context and in a confrontational, way that screams—too much information.

In our quest for meaning in a world seemingly devoid of it, we embrace movements like "local" food and a return to such traditional values and activities as gardening, food preservation, and quilting. We long for the good old days, masked by the saccharine sweetness that accompanies the passage of time. The good old days were—on close examination—not the good old days at all, but they represent something we willingly gloss over to find peace. We seek meaning in favor of the cold flickering computer screen in the middle of the night. We reach collectively for the lifeboat, the message, and the inspiration to know that we are in safe harbor.

In these pages, I could walk through a litany of instances in which I might have made better life and work decisions. I question whether that would be particularly helpful. All decisions are subject to human judgment and error, and mine no less or more than those of any other. The difference is that, in our current age, decisions are sliced, diced, and critiqued with a "buzzard on a carcass" mentality.

With the 24/7 media echo chamber, there is a pundit on every street corner to second-guess everything. Moreover, that pundit might be the one whose message will catch on and go viral. I concluded that even the pundits would have difficulty poking holes in, and deflating, my sense of self-worth when the decisions I make are right and ethical. Handling the aftermath of any disaster with grace is difficult. Learn not to care as much about what others think. What is important is that you are at peace with your life choices.

Handling flying coconuts with grace is anticipating and preparing for the world in which you live. Learn to live your life by making good, balanced decisions. Learn to make decisions with the comfort that you did so according to a set of values and principles produced by greater self-awareness and caring. Live within your own skin. This same self-awareness and caring can lead you through any disaster, be it sympathetic—such as a health catastrophe—or a reputation disaster, which turns you into a pariah.

The guiding principles that emerged from my journey are Humility, Hutzpah, and Humor. Paradoxical terms? Yes, on the surface. Life is full of paradox. Balance is all about juggling the sometimes disparate forces that affect us. I had to learn to cry before I could know how to laugh. I had the choice to live my life in balance, make sound decisions, and handle crisis with grace and dignity. I had the choice to lead. Leadership is about approaching each decision with the filter of doing the right thing on behalf of others, and for yourself. Think of the journey to leadership as the proper amounts of *Humility, Hutzpah, and Humor.*

Humility

Humility is fundamental to leadership and personal well-being. First, I had to embrace the stories of others that were often similar to my own, but—in most instances, more difficult. During my extensive hospital stays following the femur break and pulmonary embolism, I heard heartbreaking stories, particularly about medical disasters that were far worse than my own. I was drawn to these stories of courage. I point to those juggling multiple jobs with small children, those willing to risk their livelihood to become whistle-blowers, or the brave souls volunteering to treat patients with deadly and contagious diseases.

I discovered a second trait of humility in celebrating that our "successes" frequently stem from the support of others behind the scenes, who do not receive accolades and awards. In my case, they have been parents, grandparents, co-workers, Bernie, and my family. Rarely are we so smart that we alone are responsible for who we are and what we do. In addition, forces can work in our favor that have nothing to do with our abilities.

Airline pilot Captain Chesley B. "Sully" Sullenberger landed a jetliner on the Hudson River, in what has become known as the "Miracle on the Hudson." A number of forces including timing, weather, and, of course, his incredible steadiness all played into a successful ending. What is even more remarkable about Sully is that he didn't rest on his laurels. He has taken his brand and success to the next level by helping others achieve success, including St. Jude Children's Research Hospital. He possesses the humility to understand that using the light that shines upon him to assist others is an act of leadership.

Humility is about forgiveness. Mike Gobb could not find forgiveness, even though he had recovered from his addiction and was paying back for his transgressions. I received a letter from a friend who was incarcerated for drug offenses. With no charges for twelve years, she was recovered. Sadly, she cannot find a good job. She was seeking my help in finding one. She, too, has found no forgiveness.

By better understanding the needs of others, we are more forgiving of their decisions and less judgmental of our own. We recognize life's complications. Instead of condemning people, we mentor others and help them find their way to avoid a crisis or to dig out of one. I learned that I could live an even more meaningful life.

Jim Hunt, a former council member from Clarksburg, West Virginia, and a past president of the National League of Cities—shared with me a story of humility and redemption. Opening his door one evening, he found himself face-to-face with a former doctor from his hometown who was now delivering pizza. Jim took his pizza in awkward silence.

The doctor had completed medical school and established a family practice in a small town with a goal of helping people. In a now-too-familiar pattern, he began to self-medicate in an effort to get through days overflowing with work and family obligations. Just when he found faith and kicked his drug habit, his sloppy record keeping—no doubt brought on by his drug addiction—caught up with him.

He was convicted of Medicaid fraud and had to claw his way back to find a new life. He went from a highly successful private medical practice to pizza delivery and other odd jobs before homing in once again on his purpose to assist others. He earned his way back, not in the world of his once-lucrative private medical practice, but in a low-paying church clinic that he helped found.

According to him: "Even though I'm not making anywhere near the kind of money that I made in private practice, the quality of my life and of my relationship with my family has improved dramatically. The free time that I have now I use to connect with my loved ones, and because of that, my life is fuller and more satisfying." [14]

He is contributing more today than he likely would have done had he followed his original trajectory—a trajectory that took him away from, and not toward, his purpose. There are many doctors in the world; but few serve those in greatest need with lessons learned from their own brush with pain. I am humbled by his recovery and by what he is doing today.

Hutzpah

Hutzpah is a Yiddish term for "over-the-top" confidence. Why do I use such an outsized term? Self-confidence is required of leaders who must make tough decisions. Decisions in the line of fire often require exaggerated reaction or hutzpah. Otherwise, it would be too

---

[14] "Falling Down," Alan Dove, Ph,D., January 23, 2009

easy to walk away. Those leaders often emerge as the heroes that our times crave.

Sully, who pulled off the "Miracle on the Hudson," had the hutzpah to land an airplane on a river and the humility of empathy for the needs of others to check, not only once, but twice to ensure that all passengers were safely out before exiting and saving himself. He has emerged as a gifted and inspirational leader, who knows how to balance his hutzpah with humility.

Hutzpah is also about knowing, embracing, and boldly sharing your story, so that others may learn. Sully's books, including Highest Duty: My Search for What Really Matters, has no doubt inspired millions of people, as has Rabbi Kushner with his seminal book, *When Bad Things Happen to Good People,* concerning the ultimate crucible— the loss of a child. A true leader rises to the occasion.

In an unforgettable passage from his book, Rabbi Kushner shares his life philosophy after the loss of a child to the disease progeria, which causes rapid aging and results in early death:

> "I am a more sensitive person, a more effective pastor, a more sympathetic counselor because of Aaron's life and death than I would ever have been without it. I would give up all of those gains in a second if I could have my son back. If I could choose, I would forgo all the spiritual growth and depth which has come my way because of our experiences, and be what I was fifteen

years ago, an average rabbi, an indifferent counselor, helping some people and unable to help others, and the father of a bright, happy boy. But I cannot choose."

The loss of a child is the ultimate crucible. My experiences pale in comparison. No matter the crucible, our choice is fielding the coconut or allowing it to bludgeon us to death. Rabbi Kushner made the choice to help others understand disaster and recovery.

Humor

Humor is last. I note the power of humor, bridging humility and hutzpah, which got me through my crucibles. There is the moment with my brother taking the newspaper off the stoop and reporting that my dad had called the Herald-Leader daily for a credit on his bill. I have learned to laugh even at the cruel blog entries alluding to my ever increasingly beleaguered looks.

Humor provides the necessary salve that buffers the pain of loss and rejection and connects humility and hutzpah, two seemingly disparate qualities. Stand-up comedians are masters at taking our human weaknesses and translating them into laughter.

Humor can be found in unlikely moments, as well. My family and I stood vigil as my mother grew weak and nearly comatose from the ravages of cervical cancer; her hospital bed soon displacing the dining-room table at my parents' tiny house. With a goal of involving her in family life as the devastation of the disease and pain medication progressed, we solicited her opinions, even when she could no longer communicate effectively.

Knowing my mother had cared for my boys from the ages of 2 and 4, and was devoted to them, we took special care to involve her in their lives even as she lay dying. One afternoon—paying homage to our Scotch/Irish heritage—my aunt, a seamstress, delivered a hand-sewn kilt for Ross, my oldest son, who was then obsessed with all things Scottish. He modeled it and preened, as we all expressed admiration for Aunt Ruth's handiwork.

In an effort to draw my mother into the conversation, I asked, "Mamaw, did you see Ross's kilt?"

She turned her head toward us and, in a weak and wan voice, replied slowly: "Oh, I hope the poor little thing didn't suffer."

We realized that she had mistaken the word kilt for killed, and we roared with laughter. Not only had she misunderstood, but also her calm reaction belied what would have been her response in better times if her beloved grandson had really died. She did rally enough to express her displeasure that we found humor in the incident. The vignette survives in our family lore as a welcome memory playing against the bleak backdrop that was her suffering.

Putting the Three Hs Together

Combining humility, hutzpah, and humor is key, but how do you get there? You begin by realizing that the degree of separation among disasters is not as great as you might think. Suffering as I did, with back-to-back crucibles, is illustrative. With the reputation disaster, I was shunned—a pariah. In the aftermath of a medical disaster, I found only sympathy. The qualities that bound the two together were ending self-pity, dusting myself off, and getting back in the game. I had fallen prey to the malaise that I had it worse than did anyone else and that the world is unfair. I wanted to pick up my toys, go home, and shut myself off forever.

That is more than wrong. It is not helpful. Isolation will not solve the problem or make you feel better in the end. Blessings in this life are through interaction with people. You must get out there again. Once you master finding your core, you can move your focus from yourself to someone or something else.

Rejoining a fulfilling life is making a conscious decision to recover and give back. It is the thread that ran through my encounters with the flying coconuts. The reputation disaster taught me many things, and should be valued as an unusual and unexpected gift. I learned what truly matters. When left alone and shunned by supposed supporters and friends, I had time to contemplate.

Bitterness is the beginning, but awareness and even appreciation can come next—if you surrender. Our society places too much emphasis on the traditional trappings of success. To many of my former colleagues, I simply was of no use after my reputation disaster. I wish I had recognized their attitudes for what they were at the time. I would have known that my first duty is being of value to myself. Bottom line? I would have taken better care of myself before so investing in others.

From where and what did my journey to achieve humility, humor, and hutzpah come? As I considered all that happened to me during my year of forced contemplation, I had two goals: (1) recovering to a good and healthy life, both mentally and physically; and (2) giving back to others the lessons I learned. I was no less motivated than was Sully of Miracle on the Hudson fame, though our moments in the crucible were so dramatically different. His crucible was positive; his catcher's mitt was poised to catch the coconuts before they landed. Mine was not.

CHAPTER EIGHT

Being Ready

"A pessimist sees the difficulty in every opportunity; an optimist sees the opportunity in every difficulty."

—Winston Churchill

Thinking back to my habit of recording stories on index cards, I searched for a tool that could help busy people grasp quickly what I had learned and better their lives based on my lessons and theirs. I have long been an admirer of Carl Sagan with his groundbreaking book, Cosmos, which brought science to a broader audience and out of the musty corners of scholarly writing. The reality is that, while I love Thomas Merton and the writings of other great philosophers, their magnificent works are largely unknown. I am fortunate that Bernie exposed me to great works, and lament that others have not been so lucky.

I sought an organizational structure to help me and others understand quickly—a formula. I settled on what I call the 4P Process Purpose, Preparation, Planning, and Perspective. I knew by now that, to be balanced, I had to find the Purpose that goes to the core of who I was; I had to Prepare better by understanding the micro and macro forces in the form of coconuts flying all around me; and I had to Plan appropriately with my core intact and adaptability at the edges.

I had to embrace and understand the Perspective of Leadership, or hovering at 30,000 feet and joining the disparate pieces. The latter is important. Understanding Purpose, Preparedness, and Planning must add up to what we think of as an intangible quality of leadership. In the moment of the crucible, all that we are and have become are called into play. We do what is right and ethical, and live with the consequences of our actions. While we may not be CEO's or leaders by title or position, we all make daily decisions that affect our lives and the lives of others. Acknowledging that truth calls for leadership.

An Overview of the 4 P Process
Purpose

Get acquainted with yourself. You are stuck with you. Learn how to love the person who accompanies you daily on every decision you make. Learn what makes you tick.

Take joy in your gifts, and find humility in your limitations.

Preparation

While finding your Purpose and mission is foundational and personal, the current state of your world is critical. For this reason, Preparation involves knowing the milieu in which you operate. That includes both macro trends, which affect us all, and micro trends, which affect you in particular. Macro trends include the proliferation and overload of information; relentless change; and fear and anger at a world that is seemingly out of control.

Planning

Can we plan in a universe where it was once observed, "Instant coffee ruined the world"? Planning is actually more important in these times than it has ever been before.

Perspective

Being human is understanding that at the moment of the crucible, you do have a choice. Sully could have made a different decision when he landed the airplane on the Hudson River. He checked the plane twice, making sure all the passengers were evacuated. He made a choice to provide leadership when needed..

Even with the Perspective of Leadership, where we hover at 30,000 feet, we can still make wrongheaded decisions. Those who don't bother to examine the circumstances can misconstrue our decisions. Learning to live with what may not be a Hollywood ending is a valuable skill.

Lessons Learned:

- Be at peace with who you are.
- Stop the pity party; others likely have it much worse than you do.
- Collect your stories and those of others.
- Acquire Humility, Hutzpah, and Humor—all in balance.

CHAPTER NINE

Purpose

"A man left his house every day in the wee hours to visit his nursing home bound wife stricken with Alzheimer's. A neighbor asked him one morning: 'Why do you visit her each day when she no longer knows who you are?' 'Because I know who I am' was his reply."

—Author unknown

Do I know the answer to the question, "Who am I?" Am I not the one person with whom I should be most acquainted? We do not, given the eagerness with which we embrace such personality-inventory tests as Myers-Briggs and read *What Color Is Your Parachute?* More and more employers utilize such "inventories" of personality to make hiring choices that fit into their culture.

I, too, developed a keen interest in these personality inventories following my crucibles. Perhaps like so many others, I am searching for a sense of core being in a world of flying coconuts, which take the form of fragmented messages and confusion. At the request of our son Ross, I recently picked up *Please Understand Me*, a book described as an exploration of character and temperament types, by David Keirsey and Marilyn Bates. Ross, who had taken the 70-question personality inventory test, was anxious for me to do the same.

The questions are tortuous. With each question, I would think, "I'm like this, but then sometimes … I'm like that." Conventional wisdom says the best answer is the first answer that comes to mind. Of course, if we do not like the results, we find comfort in the fact that we can take it again and change the score. Would the results be different if it is a sunny day or a rainy one? We know our moods change; so do our responses to personality inventories.

The test is informative. It is fun to take it and then compare the results and the insights with fellow test takers, particularly with family members because they share our history.

What I did not confess to my son was that I always end up on the cusp of types. By this, I mean that—on a given day—I can be an extrovert, an introvert, or a combination of the two. One test administrator even suggested that I must have been going through trauma that accounted for a "somewhat schizophrenic response." Of course, the actual trauma was to come much later.

I note that I am excellent at working a room and sneaking quickly out the backdoor to find some alone

time. I like being with, and interacting with, anyone—
even strangers—but not for long. Is that introversion,
extroversion, or some new personality species that I have
invented?

That description of my "type" (as assessed on this
particular day) struck us both as entertaining. My official
"label" doesn't matter. Like a horoscope, my type description is laden with positives and a sense of unique-
ness. I was "an excellent homemaker" and "possessed of
a well-kept home, meticulously maintained and appointed."

That description sent my son into gales of laughter,
so much so that it made me uncomfortable. Make no
mistake, I was never a good housekeeper and did not give
a fig about how my home décor. He no doubt remem-
bers that well. I was the traveling mom, often missing
milestones in my sons' lives. I recall a photo of David
taken at a Halloween party. He was dressed as a cowboy,
and Ross wore a space-alien costume. I experienced that
event in their lives only through the picture. I was away at
a meeting, discussing a problem that no longer matters.

Knowing that our priorities change with circum-
stance and experience, I wonder if I was answering the
quiz in a way that reflected my attempt to rewrite history.
The resulting description of my personality type indicated
that I had a great desire to be of service and to minister
to the needs of others, along with a strong sense of "history and tradition. My type is hardworking and believes
that playtime must be earned. All this fits me like a glove.
On an interesting note, the description included a reluc-

tance to "boss" others. Ross had grown up seeing me in the role of boss, a role in which he thought I found comfort. What he never realized was my discomfort and the war that raged within me about direction—to pursue eclectic interests, such as writing, or to be a big time, in-charge CEO.

Circumstances gladly made that decision for me. I was a chameleon and an adapter ... perhaps to a fault. I acquired this trait from my father. On a final note, the description indicated that my personality type is often underappreciated. That has elicited more than one LOL from a family member.

Stages of life can affect our assessments. At one time, looking fashionable meant more to me than it does now. What do I need with one more jacket or another piece of jewelry? I have plenty. The famous newscaster, Greta Van Susteren, once shared her New Year's resolution with her audience: to comb her hair before going on camera, instead of afterward.

Of late, I have had to remind myself to check my look before going out, for fear of resembling a bag lady pushing a grocery cart full of cans. I still realize a need to fit into the mainstream, but not allowing artificial boundaries to compromise who I am, even if what I am is complicated.

One joyful outcome of my taking the test is that Ross learned more about me through the simple act of taking a personality-inventory test than he had growing up in the same house with me. He can now take that knowledge in his thirties, process it, and implement it as a

piece of his own tapestry and growth. We owe that to our
children and others. Think of a personality-inventory test
as just one more "fun" tool that can help you and others
know you better.

Knowing who you are lies at the base of understanding your purpose and mission. In its November 2014 edition, *Fast Company* magazine features Robert Safian's
article titled, "Generation Flux's Secret Weapon." The
article weaves together movements and trends that offer
a window into how we live and work.

Flux, which is about state of mind rather than
chronological age, is about finding your purpose and mission to have a meaningful life and career. So, what are the
interests of "Generation Flux"? On a personal level, they
include the desire to live a meaningful life that transcends
monetary rewards. The trend among those "fluxers" in
corporate America is to move away from obsession with
shareholder rewards and reach consumers and others by
reaffirming authenticity and trust. Values are front and
center, along with a sense of a greater societal purpose.
Sallie Krawcheck, who is profiled in the Safian article,
shares survey results showing that "Gentlemen," when
asked what is most important to them in work life, say
money is number one. Women rank money as number
four, while "meaning and purpose" are number one.

Robert Putnam's observations in his book, *Bowling
Alone*, are that we have the ability to acquire "friends"
with the click of a mouse, but ironically, we are actually
more alone than ever. We engage in activities, like bowl-

ing, but increasingly not with friends or family—but alone.

Our desire for lives that are more satisfying and integrated with human community spills over into the workplace. We refuse to leave our lives at the office door on Monday morning. I learned that work and life should be seamless—our need for community and human interaction paramount.

We see the rapid growth of farmers' markets frequented for fresh food. They increasingly serve as places where we meet with friends and neighbors. Could it be that, because the hand that delivers the bag of tomatoes is weatherworn with dirt-crusted fingernails, it becomes as important as the bag and its contents? Is trust restored through this simple act?

William H. Whyte's book, *The Organization Man*, made waves in the 50s with its portrait of the typical professionally employed "man." He came to work in a crisp white shirt and navy suit and adhered to the rules—flying under the radar and never, ever talking back to the boss or making waves. We now question this paradigm and hope that greater employee pushback will lead to more creativity in the workplace.

I, along with so many others, have become an independent contractor—a trend that leaves me with a sense of being in charge of my own destiny. However, it also denies me the security that my father enjoyed making registers and being cared for by a paternalistic employer. Near the end, even he realized that job security held only a brief moment in the sun during the years of the post-WWII boom.

Descriptive buzzwords litter the world. I found that those words reflect reality. Trust in once-revered institutions—such as government, corporations, and employers—has evaporated. However, there is good. The whole idea of who is or is not smart is turned on its head.

My favorite television situation comedy is "The Big Bang Theory", featuring four geeky, but genius men and a "smarter-than-any-of-them," community-college dropout, Penny. While waitressing at night, she is pursuing her dream of becoming a Hollywood star. By contrast, the "guys" all hold high-paying jobs and advanced science degrees. There is no definition of success (except income, which is woefully ill-distributed) that reflects a meaningful and successful life.

Knowing who you are is part gift and part skill, with some of us being better at it than others are. Some of us are born with a keen sense of purpose and self; others must acquire it through environmental forces, like upbringing and experience. Some reject who they are in favor of who they would like to be. Some fail dramatically and commit grievous errors, including a turn to drugs and alcohol in an attempt to be something they are not. I remember the stories about the president of MSU; standing up to the bullying board member; and about Sybylla, in the movie My Brilliant Career, who—despite the odds—pursues her calling to write, instead of compromising into marriage to a wealthy suitor.

The idea of purpose and mission is not new, but is becoming more popular in today's challenged world. Many complain that searching for "purpose" and "mission" can get us deeply in debt to narcissism—that a "me" society is already raging. Why be obsessed with knowing even more about yourself?

One question nagged at me as I considered Purpose as the linchpin of my formula for living in this chaotic age. Was I encouraging narcissism in others and myself in this age of "selfies"? I scrambled for the dictionary. Narcissism is defined as an unhealthy obsession with oneself—something that was never my intent. I talked to others about my dilemma.

One young woman shared with me that she was giving up Facebook, as if relinquishing a drug habit. She was "overwhelmed" by the braggarts, book-signing announcements, and honors received. She felt inadequate in the face of all these supposed successes, which were part of the marketing, branding, and self-promotional campaigns of the average Facebooker or solopreneur. She wanted to drop out; find her own level without being forced to compare herself with others, who were seemingly so much more successful. I think she is onto something.

As I listened to her, I made note of the social-media revolution and evolution. Facebook usage has a generational bent. As it gains ground among older friends, young people move on to new and different platforms reflecting generation changeover from the baby boomer to the millennial set.

Expect more disruption to social media as the generational changeover continues. We do not know what will
come about to take the place of what is going on today.
Millennials represent one of the largest generations to
take its place as prime spenders with 92 million among its
cohort compared to baby boomers with 77 million.[15] The
US Bureau of Labor and Statistics reports that Millennials
(those born between 1980 and 2000) will dominate the
workforce by a 75 percent majority by the year 2030.
They will shape the world in ways we cannot imagine.

My young friend is not alone in growing weary of
current media outlets and in seeking a more rewarding
way of life. Studies show that 50 percent of Millennials
say they are more likely to buy a brand they know supports a cause.[16] They are more likely to question company
ethics and are more aware of conservation organizations
and the idea of giving back.

Relentless change is always just around the corner.
Like me, you may belong more to the "facelift" crowd
than you do to the "Facebook" crowd. In any case, be-
ware of the dangers and opportunities presented by ever
evolving social media, and distinguish between the two.
More and more users are employing the medium not only
to promote themselves, which you may or may not welcome, but to tell a story and create experiences for others.

Being in the restaurant business, I know how one
bad review, whether real or made-up, can prove devastat-

---

[15] www.goldmansachs.com/our-thinking/pges/millennials/
[16] Fromm & Garton, 2013

ing. On the other hand, offering a glimpse into the kitchen of my restaurant and featuring a photo of one of the cooks is delightful and creates opportunities to share stories and experiences with others. Bottom line? Understanding and utilizing new media tools does not mean you are a narcissist. Like so many things in life, balance is the key. As Ben Franklin, the American statesman once said, "Moderation in all things ... including moderation."

Thus, while Purpose is not narcissism, you must be vigilant. As a child, I would watch as my mother nurse a tiny abandoned bird back to health and released into the wild. I noted her care not to squeeze and harm the baby bird, but at the same time to hold on tightly enough to feed a squirming tiny creature from a doll-sized bottle. Likewise, by understanding yourself and the world around you, and by focusing on who you are in relation to others, you will connect with your "meaning," your gifts, and your limitations.

Competition

Being competitive and buying into a "rat race" of accomplishments, I would often measure my success against that of others. Following my crucibles, I know that my story is unique to me. I have stopped comparing myself to others who inhabit the worlds that are no longer mine.

This is embodied in the young woman's concern about Facebook entries. The message? When comparing your accomplishments with those of others, know that they will always be in a different place than you are. He or she may be more successful in a traditional sense, give better speeches, or write more and better books. There is an element of luck or knowing the right people—or perhaps it is just the mystery of the universe that finds you where you are now. Embrace it.

Rejoice in your own accomplishments, but take pleasure and celebrate the accomplishments of others. Turn it around: Instead of fearing the person you think is "ahead" of you, use him or her as your role model. At one time, that person was right where you are now or has an unhealthy need to puff up his or her accomplishments. Jealousy is a negative emotion, which will yield negative energy. You do not need it.

I not only read—but practically devoured—memoirs and read hundreds of comeback stories during my year of forced contemplation. I found some of them off-putting. with advice for "finding oneself" in weekly sessions with a yoga master or through monthly stays at the condominium on the beach, or the ones within sight of majestic mountains from the vantage point of Aspen, Colorado.

Why? I have no trust fund; or an excess of free time for weekly visits to a professional for advice on "finding myself"; nor the ability to travel on a whim to a resort. If you are not famous or wealthy, (most of us are not), what do you do? I begin with the advice given to me by the mayor who suggested that I maintain a file of index cards, where I record the stories of the remarkable people whom I meet on my life journey. Today, such activity may seem anachronistic—who keeps notes on index cards when computers and iPhones, which can record pictures and text, are at our fingertips? I still prefer index cards that I carry around with me. I don't have to find a keyboard. I can reach for one of about 40 pens and pencils that find their way to the bottom of my outsized purse.

My index cards are the beginning of an activity that I call journaling, which is foundational to finding Purpose. It is gaining popularity, and a computer, notebook, or index cards are all you need. There is no necessity for a yoga mat or a visit to the Dalai Lama. It is gaining in popularity for the same reasons that I started to record stories. The world has become an "in-your-face" bewilderment. Our exposure to information is too vast and chaotic to allow us to sift through and grasp what is important or truthful. That is why journaling has become more popular as a tool for grabbing hold of something and feeling its message.

Journals have become both verb and noun. I will refer to both, but prefer the more active verb because I want to think of journaling as reflecting active participation, whereas "journals" can be stodgy, boring, and relegated to the background.

Journaling can preserve our stories and our history. One person found his great-grandmother's journal in the attic of the old family homestead. It was a complete account of how the family lived in the nineteenth century. She wrote about the family trip to the general store and the exact measurements of flour, sugar, and other staples. She related how the proprietor would record the purchases and collect payment when the tobacco was harvested and sold. It made his great-grandmother come alive for him!

Like old photos, journaling provides a narrative of our unique and shared histories and of ways that our lives have changed and yet stayed the same. It is a companion to the current craving for such websites as Ancestry.com, from which we seek out our ancestors in desperation to moor ourselves to the more solid rock of knowing who we are and that our lives matter.

I take a moment each day to record a thought—perhaps a fleeting one that exemplifies leadership. Just recently, I noted an interview with former Senator and one-time aspiring presidential candidate, Bob Dole. In the AARP Magazine, he mentioned his World War II injury, which rendered his left arm useless. It happened in Italy just one day before the war ended.[17]

He lamented only briefly about what might have been had the war ended just one day earlier. He then re-called that his Armenian surgeon refused to accept pay-ment for the multiple surgeries and advised him to "make the most of what he had left," despite his grievous injury. We have to admit he did just that. I take that message to heart and have it recorded for myself and others to al-ways remember.

In an effort to progress beyond my index cards, I enrolled in a community-education course on journal writing from David Dick, a famed journalist who had retired to Kentucky, his native state. I have one great take-away from that course. "Don't turn journaling into

---

[17] AARP magazine, July/August 2015, Vol. 56, No. 6.

yet another chore in a long list of to do's," he told us. We all have those lists, and Mr. Dick knew that if something had to go, it would not be that report due tomorrow to your boss or taking your child to soccer practice. It would be your journal.

He suggested we set aside time each day, even ten minutes, to write an entry in a dedicated notebook. Make the entry no more than one page. I became more disciplined in my writing by following his counsel. Always in a hurry to get Phoenix out the door or to get somewhere, I can go quickly to my index cards to record a brief thought. Later, when I have time I can explore that thought in my journal. All it takes to pique my interest is a particularly striking news item or a personal observation.

I wrote recently about the birth of Jack, my latest grandson, during the rainiest summer in memory. I plan to tease him someday that he brought the monsoons with him. Just imagine his joy at finding this journal entry as a celebration of his life and arrival. It might even provide him with a clue as to who he is and his fit in the world.

I hear prospective journal writers complain that they are not writers and do not have intriguing lives, worthy of "journaling." I tell them that we are all writers and storytellers, and that all our stories are interesting. Some of us have more technical writing skills than do others, but all have fascinating stories about which to write. Unfortunately, the world of today has separated the rest of us from the celebrities about whom we know too much.

Ordinary is okay. I am not a Hollywood sensation and I will never achieve that level of fame. I rejoice in my ordinariness. If I were living a normal life, then an exciting one would likely be too much for my heart to take. I embrace that I am living a spectacular springboard into appreciating my gifts … and limitations.

One last piece of advice is, "Don't edit your journal." You will note that I share journal entries recorded during my year of forced contemplation. I take care not to edit my thoughts. I would like to keep them pure as reflecting the raw, happy, or sad emotions that were with me at the time. If you obsess about editing, you will lose interest and give up journaling. Moreover, you will overlook the raw feeling that brought the entry to mind. There is beauty in imperfection, like appreciating the mutt you picked out at the dog pound with one blue and one brown eye, the body of a dachshund, and the head of a beagle. It is a humbling reminder that we are human, and our thoughts are not always neatly packaged.

Explore questions: Where are your parents from? What trials and tribulations did they face? What is the one thing you remember that made your parents angry with you? Where or to whom do you turn to for advice in the moment of crisis? What was your greatest moment of triumph, or of sadness? The questions are endless, and the answers will supply stories and learning opportunities.

It is never too late to begin journaling. It is ideal to start young. I note on Facebook that many young people are sharing stories and pictures of loved ones and of experiences. I fear that this is, in some cases, dangerously close to narcissism, but, on the other hand, it offers a path to greater understanding of how the threads of their history come together to make them what they are. I prefer the more private recording of thoughts.

You enter into the world of journaling without prejudice. Your story is uniquely yours, as seen through your eyes and through the reflections of others around you. My growth in journaling happened when I expanded beyond recording the stories of the remarkable mayors whom I met through my work at KLC. I began to write more than about the people I met, and my thoughts on their fit in the world. You come to better understand your own foibles; moments of crisis and triumph; those of others; and how they all connect in a life well lived.

Pay particular attention to acquiring greater understanding of the role that others play in your life. Who are your mentors? What traits do they possess that are worth adopting? What qualities do they have that you admire? Perhaps you know someone who failed in some way or suffered a tragedy—how was he or she able to pick up and move on with grace? What can we learn from his or her life experience? What are the bonuses of overcoming tragedy? You will have a new appreciation not only for yourself, but also for the amazing people who touch your life.

A Summary of My Advice:
- Set aside time each day to journal.
- Limit your journal entry to one page in length.
- Do not edit your entry.

- Think of your life story as the fascinating one that it is. What do you want to know about yourself and others in your life? What are the stories of your heroes?
- Know that it is never too late to begin to journal.
- Be confident in your story, and do not worry about the technicalities of writing.

Companions to Journaling

Journaling serves as the linchpin to identifying Purpose. Journaling opens the door to discovering your core strengths. It came naturally to me when my crucibles tore down my inhibitions. My writings helped me understand the paradox of recognizing my significance, despite my ordinariness. However, journaling is not the only path to finding Purpose. It can be done in other ways.

Self-Care

Before I was "felled" by the flying coconuts, my life consisted of moving at breakneck speed to meet all my obligations—serving as a CEO of a major statewide association, co-parenting two young boys, and caring for aging parents. In retrospect, I realize that I did not do any one of those tasks as well as I should have. I am not alone. Many of us are guilty of over-commitment and of settling for doing less than our best.

An up-and-coming movement in corporate and nonprofit environments is "self-care." Taking care of yourself not only makes you better able to assist others, but it allows you the opportunity to reflect on your own gifts and limits. Workshops, retreats, seminars, and for-profit businesses are springing up with the objective of teaching tired and weary souls the fundamentals of self-care.

I have attended many of these workshops and vow to do more self-care, whether in organized classes or on my own. Even with my life today outside the rat race of career achievement, I find that my days are filled with obligations—to my restaurants, to my clients, and to my family. Self-care provides practical instructions on relaxation techniques focusing on breathing, yoga, and other methods that can be practiced anywhere—even at a desk on a busy workday. Using simple techniques, self-care can be learned and nurtured. The key to self-care is realizing that no one is immune to the ravages of busy, chaotic times. I sometimes perform self-care by just taking a deep breath before pondering a solution to a vexing problem.

When faced with one of those problems, I ask the question, "What really makes a positive difference in my life?" The simple answers are my family and core work. The rest—travel, events, clothes—are all just icing on the cake if they come at all. If a client is less than pleased, or if I say hurtful words to someone, I can always say, "I'm sorry." Doing so is not painful, though most of us avoid the phrase like the plague. As long as I am intact at my core and Purpose, then I can survive the frequent interruptions that come with a busy life.

Mindfulness

Mindfulness is a growing discipline that leads to better balance and therefore the ability to focus on Purpose.

In my case, mindfulness recognizes the force of the coconuts that were flying all about me, while allowing me to retain my sense of self. If I had done so, I would have fielded those coconuts that I could, and would have reacted to the others with a calm spirit. I would have accepted what I could change and left to the universe what I could not. As Charlie Brown responded—with exasperation and, ultimately, peace—upon being told about the billions of stars and planets in the universe, "I love my dog." I needed to find a path amidst chaos to my inner self. I needed to love me.

The popular magazine, *Psychology Today*, defines mindfulness as "a state of active, open attention on the present." When mindful, I note that I am not engaging in second-guessing. I am prepared, make a decision, and am at peace. I observe thoughts and feelings without judging them. Instead of letting my life pass me by, I live in the moment and get the most out of my experiences.[18]

Meditation

The Mayo Clinic describes meditation as a pathway to relaxation and stress relief. Mayo staff writers point out that meditation—practiced for thousands of years—was originally, and is still today, employed as a pathway to understanding the spiritual meaning of life. The teachings of meditation require focus that shuts out the noise and allows for fielding the coconuts. According to some medical professionals, it yields physical as well as spiritual

---

[18] www.psychologytoday.com/basics/mindfulness

benefits, especially those related to the cardiovascular system.[19]

Faith

The role of faith in Purpose is personal to each of us. Like many others, I do not participate in formal church attendance, but believe in the peace of spirituality that comes with believing in a force greater than my own. A turn to faith, however practiced, is part of many spiritual movements that seek to ground us and serve to make sense out of all those coconuts hurtling our way. I know many whose faith has gotten them through their crucible and allowed them to recover with grace, dignity, and a strong sense of self. Humility, which is a major tenet of religion, is vital to understanding and embracing Purpose. The humble acceptance of our limits and a value system that puts caring for yourself and others above ambition lies at the center of much religious dogma.

Other Ways

Safian's *Fast Company* magazine article features Eileen Fisher, the successful iconic fashion designer, and her purpose chair.[20] Fisher is determined to make a positive difference both personally and professionally. During a retreat with her executive staff, the facilitator instructed her to sit on a stool and consider how her personal purpose connected to her company's purpose.

---

[19] www.medicalnewstoday.com; February 26, 2014
[20] "Generation Flux's Secret Weapon" | *Fast Company* | Business; www.fastcompany.com/3035975/generation.

Today, she reports that when she perceives a threat to her personal or professional well-being, she retreats to her "purpose" chair. It has become her "place" to contemplate the company's and her purpose with positive results for both.

Through a purpose chair or other means, we can delve within ourselves in simple, inexpensive ways. This process is intensely personal. My own sense of a purpose chair is finding a time in my day for a moment to reflect on what is important. When I have faced a crisis, I remind myself of what matters. I was fired in a very public way from my dream job. I survived. I still have my family and friends and that is what is important.

My advice is to accept and embrace a purpose chair in your own way, no matter how odd or eccentric your choice may seem to others. In Heather Lende's memoir, *Take Good Care of the Garden and the Dogs*, she describes the joy of being alone and doing nothing—to her that means taking a walk in her Alaska forest, singing at the top of her lungs. [21] It may be something completely different for you. A willingness to stand in that place while appreciating yourself is the point.

I am captivated with the movie *The Wizard of Oz* and by its connection to the sense of place and purpose in our lives. Filmed in 1939, this story possesses transcendent themes that appeal to children and adults alike. I often watch movies and write about the characters who

---

[21] *Take Good Care of the Garden and the Dogs: A True Story of Bad Breaks and Small Miracles*; Lende, Heather, April, 2011.

triumph over adversity with their courage and integrity. I am particularly interested in those who lose their way, but despite the odds, find home base. Thus lies my interest in Dorothy's journey.

Dorothy's story begins with her dissatisfaction with living on a Kansas farm as an orphaned girl with her Auntie Em and Uncle Henry. Dorothy runs away from home and meets a fortune-teller. He convinces her to return to the farm by telling her that Auntie Em is sick with worry. With the wind of an approaching tornado buffeting her, she returns to find that no one is there. Auntie Em, Uncle Henry, and their three farmhands have all taken refuge in the storm shelter after a frantic and fruitless search for Dorothy.

Along with her dog Toto, Dorothy manages to enter the farmhouse, only to be knocked unconscious and hit by a flying window. She awakens to find herself in the Land of Oz, which is a place of unusual color, beauty, adorable munchkins, and both a good and bad witch.

"The Good Witch" tells her she must find the great and powerful Wizard of Oz to return to Kansas but along the way, she must first confront the Wicked Witch. Along the way, she meets a Scarecrow looking for a brain, a Cowardly Lion seeking courage, and a Tin Man desiring a heart. All eerily resemble the three farmhands back home.

Together, Dorothy and her friends destroy the Wicked Witch. They become the heroes of Oz. Finally arriving at the Emerald City, they are told by the towns-people of Oz that the "great and powerful" wizard can grant them their heart's desire. The Wizard, who hides behind a curtain, is cranky and clearly not happy to see them.

When the curtain is pushed back, it reveals the fake wizard. He is only a tired old man, speaking into a microphone and pulling levers. He, too, is from Kansas and anxious to return home in the hot air balloon that delivered him, after blowing him off course, to Oz. The citizens of Oz revere him as the answer to their problems, but his heart's desire is only to be relieved of the burden of being a wizard.

In one last act of kindness—if not wisdom—before leaving, he manages to make the wishes of Dorothy's companions come true. He presents a diploma to the Scarecrow; a medal of valor to the Lion; and a heart-shaped watch, complete with ticking sounds, to the Tin Man.

He then turns to Dorothy, who pronounces in a voice drained of hope and belief in dreams coming true, "There's nothing in that black bag for me."

He assures Dorothy that the hot-air balloon will do the trick and invites her to accompany him. Before the balloon can take flight, Toto runs away, and Dorothy goes in chase. The balloon leaves both Dorothy and Toto behind. Despondent, she believes that she will never return home. Glinda, the Good Witch, suddenly appears with a revelation.

Glinda explains to Dorothy that she has always had the power to go home. She had to come to know it within herself. Glinda asks Dorothy, "What have you learned?"

"I've learned ... that it wasn't enough to want to see Uncle Henry and Auntie Em ... and that if I ever go looking for my heart's desire again, I shouldn't look any further than my own backyard. Because if it isn't there, then I never really lost it to begin with. Is that right?" Dorothy did not need the Wizard after all.

Dorothy clicks her heels together three times, chanting, "There's no place like home. There is no place like home. There's no place like home." She awakens in her home in the loving company of Auntie Em, Uncle Henry, Toto, and the three farmhands.

Home Base Is You

Home base is what your Purpose is all about both in your personal and professional life. Finding home base earlier—rather than later—is ideal but, in my case, finding it at the age of 60 worked out fine. Arriving at your Purpose and knowing who you are will provide the buffer between the pain and angst that are inevitable in our lives.

I learned:

- While I got a late start in learning great lessons of life, I know that it was not too late.
- Knowing myself is not narcissism, but a healthy development of my core-self.
- Journaling helps me to understand my story. It helps me see how it relates to the lives of others.
- I must be vigilant in my efforts to stay

grounded and know always how to return to home base.

CHAPTER TEN

Preparation

"I try hard to be cynical...but it is so hard
to keep up."

—Lily Tomlin

I found that reaching within for peace was not
enough. Engagement in a sometimes unwelcoming outside world was equally important in preventing me from
becoming so gummed up inside that I would never leave
the cocoon of my own thoughts and opinions. What I
discovered was unpleasant. With world forces boiling, we
are driven under the nearest rock, where hope cries out
for an "all clear" that never comes. As the president of
the "I-know-too-much-club," I know that the next step
can be cynicism or mistrust and lack of belief in just
about everything. I do not want to go there.

I recall in my halcyon days arranging visits with the
governor to hear stories and requests of the "hopeful." I
would gladly comply with these requests. Then, I would

sit back and watch while this supplicant beggar, oozing with sincerity, poured out her soul for a worthy cause. Then I, and only I, would note the governor's furtive glance at his watch as he nodded in agreement. Clearly, he had tuned out long before that.

He was practiced in the art of politics, and knew how to "appear" intent and caring. I didn't know whether to laugh or to cry. Although politics was a huge part of my career, I dangerously gravitate toward intolerance for it. However, I quickly realized that was the system to bring needed change to the world.

The world that I faced during my recovery appeared insincere, shallow, and often horrific. While we can oppose and push for change, we work within that which is in place, both good and bad, to achieve peace and balance from within. Knowing what is going on around you is helpful; cynicism is toxic.

I am not suggesting that you become a news junkie, planning your day around the ever-present cable "breaking news" and blaring dramatic musical accompaniments. Quite to the contrary, becoming a news junkie will likely lead to cynicism. Much of the 24-hour news cycle is garbage. I would never suggest that watching beheadings on YouTube.com would add up to a life well lived.

To be prepared, I had to understand both the macro and micro forces that were swirling around me and apply them to my life without succumbing to self-pity, paranoia, and the "life-is-unfair" syndrome. By comprehending trends and undercurrents of change in the world, I am in an education and awareness campaign that will never end.

Macro forces are those bombarding all of us regardless of our walk of life. They include the sheer volume of information; its delivery in new and multiple ways; and instantaneous communications. Growing up, I was privy to only three-television channels—-NBC, CBS, and ABC. I can fragment my viewing interest today not just on multiple news channels, but choose which pundit can provide me the "expert" opinion I prefer.

A downed airliner becomes 72 hours of nonstop news no matter where it happens and includes gory detail, along with poignant life stories that could be about us. These macro forces change our behaviors and us in profound ways. Among those forces are the growing anonymity and untrustworthiness of our interactions with one another through automated transactions, security breaches, and the depiction of violence streaming from across the world onto our media devices. The world grows scarier and scarier as we lose the ability to believe in almost anything.

Computers and big data, while valuable on one level, are nonetheless dehumanizing our jobs and compromising our ability to communicate face-to-face in the most human of ways. My father's years spent at NCR marked the end of the industrial age, during which many hands toiled to make the goods that Americans wanted and needed.

My father lost his job to automation, which heralded the exchange of human hands and machines for robots and computers. It served to further separate our handi-work and us from one another. My father never found a job to replace the one he lost at NCR. As I have noted, near the end of his life, he complained bitterly, "those computers put me out of work." He did not live to witness the all-encompassing role that computers would come to play in our lives, both good and bad. Those of us who are alive today will not live to get a glimpse of what is to come.

My father railed in anger, feeling helpless and impotent to stop the relentless "progress" that had overtaken his life. We are currently facing the second wave of computer supremacy. Computers are increasingly replacing not just factory workers, but other white-collar and high-skill-level, blue-collar positions. Knowing and understanding the world today is key to our survival, our security, and our happiness.

Digging deeper, I ask this question: Is the world more sinister and barbaric today than ever before? Why should we ask and answer that question? In his book, *One Summer*, Bill Bryson profiles the tumult of the summer of 1927. It is a micro-snapshot of the era. Babe Ruth broke baseball records, and Lindbergh flew across the Atlantic as America faced a seemingly bright and limitless future. But it was also an era during which Sacco and Vanzetti were executed more for being Italian than for the robbery, for which scant evidence was produced, to prove their guilt. It was an era when Al Capone was shooting up Chicago.

The world is not more sinister and barbaric today. The answer is important for tamping down growing cynicism. Quite simply, we know more than ever before in a news/entertainment format that furnishes "news," often without context. By knowing more, we meet with more rules and wires over which to trip in our daily lives. In the age of hyper-transparency, nothing you have ever done or to which you reacted is hidden from anyone who is savvy enough to Google your name. Again, whether yours is a crucible related to a reputation disaster; a decision made in the moment of crisis; or a health or other personal crisis, being prepared is essential. As society seeks to harness the nearly uncontrollable barrage of information, the new rules provide the trip wire. Coupled with the downfall of traditional media is the hunger for multiple outlets to "tell the story." Anyone with a mouse and computer is an investigative reporter, and any real or perceived transgression can go viral in an instant.

A print-newspaper editor, in a lecture on the changing world of journalism, pointed out that, if a meteor crashed into earth in the parking lot next to the meeting room, the traditional news media would not arrive at the scene first. Seminar participants would be first on the scene, cellphones ablaze, along with tweets and other social media postings, all with their own interpretation of what had happened.

There is not necessarily anything wrong with these "new" rules. They merely represent the state of the world as it is. We have barely enough time to digest what is going on and improve it before change happens again.

Change is relentless and gives us little reaction time. We constantly try to find ways to stem the tide and enhance our lives through rules.

Micro Trends

Micro trends are those that influence your work and life circumstances. Given my career with elected officials, I should have had greater awareness of what politics meant to my well-being. Even though it was my professional playing field, I missed the signals. I failed to consider that local officials had a higher calling than defending me when the crucible came.

Their livelihood and calling was keeping potholes filled and garbage collected. How could defending me compare with a simple service mission: making sure the "trains arrive on time" and that they are re-elected? That was a valid choice on their part, and it did not contain any ill will toward me. It was my problem. To believe otherwise was not based on reality.

I was scolded by one mayor, to whom I was extolling the virtues of pursuing my visionary dream of lifting cities up in the eyes of the media and the public for a state that was stuck in a rural paradigm. He stopped me in midsentence with this warning: "Don't get too far ahead of me, little lady."

His message is clear to me now. I should have paid closer attention. Being re-elected was paramount in his mind and in that of my other elected officials, and media endorsements are critical. In the end, I had become a liability to that higher calling. Perhaps that explains the sudden amnesia that afflicted many of the mayors who had participated in, and, along with me, made the critical decisions that brought me down.

Once the coconuts started to fly, a number of the decisions that my board made were suddenly cast as "my" decisions. The universal truth is that, when the crucible comes, memories are short and self-serving. There is no greater loneliness than being the person in charge during or after the fall. Know and understand those micro trends impacting you.

A Clear Understanding

It is better to be prepared by documenting decisions that are made before the scrutiny begins and information, some true and some not, is flying around. I was hired with a handshake. An employment contract, with an exit strategy, would have been better.

A foundational principle of business ... any business, is this: "Clear communication makes for good business." This means that it is vital to understand your job, your responsibilities, and what is expected of you prior to accepting a position. The best way to ensure that is in writing. If I had had an employment contract, perhaps a more graceful "exit strategy" would have been possible and saved the board and me heartache and embarrassment.

I recall one staff member approaching me on what was likely one of my darkest days. I do not recall the exact "Sylvia" news story of the day, but I know I was deep into my depression. She was angry and stalked into my office with these words: "Why didn't you follow the crisis plan we had prepared for this moment?" I began to weep and, rather than offering me comfort, she merely stalked out of the room.

I look back now and know that my weakness was not providing the comfort she needed. I also know after reviewing her "crisis" plan, though, that it described what to do in the case of a natural disaster, such as a tornado or flood. It was about getting people out of the building and making them physically safe. There was no plan for "political" crisis or the leadership crisis in which we found ourselves. That requirement had never occurred to us, but it should have.

Every life story and every profession reflect micro and macro trends with which we must come to terms. Staying alert to changing political climates and changing norms is key to avoiding those flying coconuts, which can be hidden in the most mundane of activities.

Key Points to Remember

- Recognize the micro and macro trends affecting all of us in the collective and those that specifically affect you.
- Embrace your Purpose, including your gifts and limitations.
- "Trust, but verify," as the Russian proverb admonishes. It is practical.
- Know that business colleagues may feel like family ... but remember that when the coconuts begin to fly they will do what they need to do to protect themselves. There is no need to fret or to hold them in less regard; just understand.

- Inventory your preparedness, and make appropriate plans.

- Learn skills that lead to sound judgments and decisions.

- Always be the leader that you need to be.

- Prepare by understanding the macro and micro forces swirling around you.

CHAPTER ELEVEN

Planning

"All the world is a stage and most of us are desperately unrehearsed."

—Sean O'Casey

Planning follows Purpose and Preparation as the next step to well-being. I had to find a sense of Purpose, and next I needed to be Prepared. Preparation is not about 24/7 news blasts, social-media outlets, and other popular media that depress our spirit. A constant thread running through the stories about those who are at peace with themselves is that they have joy and are curious. They have a strong sense of Purpose.

As famed country singer June Carter Cash reportedly said, when asked what she was up to, "I'm just trying to matter." To be joyous and curious you must apply your Purpose and Preparation to the future for a Plan of action, which can turn the challenging moments into opportunities for living a life that matters to you and to others. You look upon the future with the optimism that enables you to face what comes.

Some say that the need for Planning has gone the way of formality. Not true. Planning is more important than ever before. As we are whipsawed by our times, we must hold firmly to our core or Purpose.

Planning, in the glare of today's micro and macro trends, is quite different than it was in the past. Gone is the old-fashioned, five-year strategic plan, from which there was no wavering. Today, the edges calling for adaptability have expanded. Plans must be adaptable to meet the needs of both your professional and personal life.

Listening to a panel of former mayors at a meeting of the National League of Cities, I was struck by their success in leading major cities, and by the common threads that made up the fabric of their leadership stories. Both Dennis Archer, former mayor of Detroit, and Henry Cisneros, former mayor of San Antonio and Department of Housing and Urban Development Secretary under President Bill Clinton, spoke about the need in our times to consider "big and small" solutions simultaneously, despite the difficulty of such a juggling act. The lesson? Do not be a slave to time, which can swallow up any effort to plan. Planning must be a deliberate act in these times of rapid change Another key lesson is to establish a vision in alignment with your Purpose and mission with the small and manageable steps that will help you achieve your goals. You follow that with regular "checkups."

Finally, acquiring skills that serve the Perspective of Leadership will get you through the inevitable crisis. In leadership, there is always a choice, sometimes easy and sometimes not. When you choose to do the right thing—not just for yourself—but for everyone involved, then you have made a solid decision. There is nothing wrong with taking care of yourself, but always keep your eye on the decision that provides the best outcomes—for everyone.

Stated simply, here are my eight steps for Purpose, Preparation, and Planning in the face of the flying coconut:

- Find your Purpose and ways to connect with yourself.
- Understand micro and macro forces affecting you and others.
- Harness time to work toward your well-being.
- Do not allow yourself to be overwhelmed.
- Discipline your mind, and stay focused.
- Develop overarching goals.
- Develop manageable steps for achieving objectives.
- Recognize your role and the need for involvement and mentoring of others.
- Be prepared to do the entire list subject to constant and regular review.

Underlying all this is the three-legged stool of humility, humor, and hutzpah. We must have the hutzpah to boldly lead, tempered with the humility to know that we are limited and enhanced by the forces of our gifts, talents, and the stories of others. Finally, humor acts as the buffer and salve of modern living. Always strive to find humor in the midst of daily chaos.

CHAPTER TWELVE

Perspective

"Man first of all exists, encounters himself, surges up in the world—and defines himself afterward."

— **Jean-Paul Sartre, French philosopher**

Jean-Paul Sartre, a French philosopher, is closely identified with the philosophy known as existentialism. Writing in the first half of the twentieth century, he explored existentialism as the uniquely human ability to make choices. This is, at the same time, a virtue and a curse. I best describe that ability to choose as "gaining Perspective."

Perspective is the human ability to lay out all that is before us, however chaotic and unreasonable, and make the best decision based on all that we know—then be at peace with yourself if it is not perfect.

Perspective is a key element of my formula due to my glaring lack of it in the moment of the crucible. In my crucible, when leadership was needed most of all, I was absent and mired down in my depression. While I was tending to my own needs for recovery, I was indulging in self-pity and "the-world-is-unfair" scenarios. I was unprepared for the leadership need that was beckoning.

Did I lack leadership qualities? Likely not. I was blessed to come face-to-face with my own demons and shortcomings. Most are not so lucky.

Our human perspective of choice demands, and depends not only on data, but on a generous helping of heart, soul, and intellect. Knowing Purpose, and having Prepared and Planned, we accept that we must make decisions, even when we do not have the luxury of time to ponder endlessly about what is right and what is wrong. Decisions are sometimes tough and complex. Hopefully, we make the right decision—but what happens when we don't? How do we live with the consequences of a bad decision, or worse yet, no decision (no decision is also a decision)? How to do we prepare ourselves to make better ones in the first place?

In our personal and professional lives, we make decisions as the crucible bears down. Having recently attended a Jewish wedding, I made note of the ritual of crushing a glass. Many theories exist about what breaking the glass symbolizes, but for me, it illustrates the young couple's responsibility to help put this chaotic world back together.

We take all that we are, hover at 30,000 feet, and see the mismatched and inexplicable puzzle pieces. We make a hasty and hopefully correct decision. As the world changes quickly, and events call for our immediate reactions, we realize that we will not always make the right choice because we are human. The agony of choice should not torment us. We choose, and then we accept. We can learn ways to be better at acquiring decision-making skills when called upon to lead.

Bernie is at peace with his airport experience. While it was bitter and negatively influenced his business and personal life, he knows he did the best he could do with what he knew at the time. Even he will offer that if he had followed the simple formula of Purpose, Preparation, Planning, and Perspective, he might have fared better as the entire airport Board might have done. Mike certainly would have benefited.

Decisions made with the best intentions, and which provide the best outcomes for all involved, should always be the goal. Borrowing the title of a provocative book by E. L. James, there are at least "Fifty Shades of Grey" to decision making. Bernie Madoff may anchor one end of the continuum, representing those who flunked the test, while Mother Teresa is on the other end.

Every true leader understands that no decision is also a decision. Anguishing endlessly and succumbing to "analysis paralysis" will not serve you well as a leader. Making a decision, based on careful consideration and good information, is always best. Above all, be willing to make decisions.

We avoid making a decision by turning inward as a protective measure. Reducing your world and making it so small that you do not have to make tough decisions is not the answer. This helps us avoid decisions, but in the end, that is turning your back on leadership. You cannot hide yourself away from facing and dealing with problems forever. The last things that we want or need are to become bitter and engage in self-pity. Burying ourselves in anger or meaningless diversions does not help. I did all that.

During my year of forced contemplation—while I was in a wheelchair, on a walker, and at various times laid out on a hospital gurney—I had time to think about my future. I thought of how I related to the world. I came to know and understand humility; to discover humor; and, with time, to find the appropriate measure of hutzpah that I had admired so much in others who had suffered greater losses. I wish that I had exhibited more hutzpah on behalf of those who depended on me for leadership.

Barbara Brown Taylor's book, *Learning to Walk in the Dark*, provides a startling new insight. While we celebrate and embrace the "light" in our life stories, we must learn to embrace the darkness. We explore the darker corners to find the appropriate amount of light for our lives and move forward. We must learn how not to stumble in the dark room full of furniture to appreciate being human and fallible.

While in the hospital drugged with Percocet, I became unusually attached to the television show "Hoarders", a reality show that explores the recognized disorder of hoarding. Hoarders are often people who have suffered serious mental trauma and have decided that collecting food, garbage, clothing, and—in some cases—animals, dead and/or alive, gives them a sense of security and protection in a chaotic world.

Episodes of "Hoarders" are sprinkled among the endless supply of cable channels, alongside "Law and Order" and many other television shows devoted to a variety of—and sometimes bizarre—slices of life. A mark of our era is the distraction we can find with the click of a mouse or a remote. We can be experts in any one topic, but increasingly lack the broader view that offers context. I would soon become an expert on hoarding.

I would stare intently as the poor broken souls would step into the spotlight before millions of viewers. It was there to elicit something … was it pity? I fell for it completely. Was it smugness that it couldn't happen to me, thus it was safe for viewing? Was it just plain voyeurism? Was it the pain medication that was altering my television tastes? I pondered my interest.

Having long ago abandoned my fascination with Hoarders, I believe an unacknowledged side of me was a hoarder. I was coming to terms with the stacks of debris in my life that I had allowed to accumulate with no examination or accounting. I had not taken the time until then to ponder my life story and how I would live out its remainder. In peace? In service to others? Are you a hoard-er, stacking and scattering your life's debris?

If I had followed my 4Ps strategy, I would have handled the moment that called for Perspective better. When the rug was pulled out from under me, I would have laid out all the options—using the information at hand—and made my decisions based on careful thought and reason. Once I made the important decisions, I could live peacefully with the consequences.

I was hired to be a decider. In the end, I shirked that responsibility, which I regret. We must accept our humanity and its gift of uncertainty in the moment of the crucible. But, we must make the decisions that are our responsibility.

As I rebuild my life and reexamine my Purpose, it is becoming clearer who I am. I am an avid student and collector of the decisions made by others as they traverse their crucible. I am humbled by the acts of leadership that make me ask, "How would I have handled that?"

Consider the story about one assistant hotel manager in a recent news story. On a beautiful and tranquil Sunday evening around 6:30, the suburban hotel was near capacity. Guests were visiting for the typical fall events of football, family reunions, and weddings. As hotel guests were getting ready for dinner in nearby restaurants, the building suddenly filled with the heavy odor of gas. I learned later that a man—intending to press the brake as he pulled up to the building—hit the accelerator in error, and crashed his car through a gas main, ending up inside the hotel.

The hotel's assistant manager, who was on duty that night, pulled the alarm. She knew, from her training as a manager, that a building filled with such strong gas vapors would eventually blow. It might take one minute or 10 minutes, but the danger to the guests and to her was imminent. She methodically knocked on each guest-room doors on all three floors, completing the evacuation.

Firefighters arrived just as the eerie creeks and pings of an impending explosion began. The building exploded minutes after being evacuated leaving only rubble. Miraculously, there were no casualties, due to quick action. When asked by a broadcast-news reporter why she risked her life to save others, she replied, "It was my training."

We marvel at the hotel manager's action. Did she think twice about how to react? Was she a single mom, who was worried that she might not make it through the crucible? Why did she risk her life? Such first responders as firefighters and police officers face similar dilemmas every day. When asked why they risked their lives for another, most first-responders answer, "It was my job." It is clear that this assistant hotel manager knew her Purpose and, through education and training, was prepared. For her, it was automatic. Her plan did not likely include this exact scenario, but she did know about its potential and therefore reacted without thinking twice. No doubt, first responders—who face crucibles on a daily basis—react in the same way.

All are susceptible to the slippery slope of bad decision making if we are not vigilant. As C. S. Lewis observed: "The safest road to Hell is the gradual one—the gentle slope, soft underfoot, without sudden turnings, without milestones, without signposts."[22]

In my reputation disaster, I had a typical, untrained human response—I shut down. I avoided bold steps. My experience came with an emerging uptick in the crisis-management movement. PR firms were grappling with the Wild West of information on the Internet. It was a growing thought that not only large corporations, but also small organizations and individuals needed to heed the movement toward transparency.

Conventional wisdom of the time of my crucible was that I not tell my side for fear it would "keep the story alive." We cannot predict in today's world when something either real or perceived will take hold. The strategy of silence was an unmitigated disaster.

My advice to any board or to any manager is based on my experiences. My board had every right to ask me to leave the organization if I had become a liability; however, it should not have happened when two reporters were outside the room.

By taking the course I did, I gave myself the opportunity to hide. I went the route of conventional wisdom, even though on some level I knew it was wrong. It was easy. Taking a stand, protecting myself and my organization, and telling my side of the story would have required me to face the crucible head-on.

---

[22] "How Unethical Behavior Becomes a Habit" by Francesca Gino, Lisa D. Ordonez, and David Welsh; Harvard Business Review, September 4, 2014.

In the end, it was not so much the confluence of circumstances that came together to spell the end of my career and cause my life-threatening depression, but instead, my untrained response. My "decision" was not to respond.

How should I have handled the flying coconut? I should have confronted the situation early on, spoken the truth, and led with confidence by gathering the facts, determining the variables and making a decision in alignment with my purpose. Aligning your decision and Purpose will guide you to the "right" decision.

Be forewarned—you are human. Decisions and judgments may not be perfect. They can be complicated, but just remember that popular book title, *Fifty Shades of Grey*. Moral choices are not always the Bernie Madoff brand of evil, but often are born out of conflict of interest and poor decisions about what is right.

To be conflicted is human, to decide is divine.

Gaining Perspective is the gift of being human. If you have ever wondered at the lack of leadership, consider the fear of judgment. In this day of instant news, so comes instant judgment. It can go viral and vicious in an instant. The paradox is that by embracing it, one embraces being human and acquires the magical combination of humility, humor, and hutzpah.

CHAPTER THIRTEEN

A Beauty No More

"Losing my timing this late in my career."

—"Send in the Clowns," by Stephen Sondheim

Mary, my then three-year-old granddaughter, was perusing an American Doll catalog photo. "Tell me the names of the beautiful ones," she insisted. "Don't tell me about the 'not' beautiful ones." She proceeded to pick and choose which ones met her standards of "beauty." Interestingly, as reflected in the toy-maker's lineup of dolls, her choices were diverse and, ultimately, her decisions were completely undecipherable. She was quickly on to something else.

I was once a "beautiful one." I was a card-carrying member of the "in crowd."

I met the standards of success that the norms of our society dictated, and I worked hard to fit in. From out of the cosmos came the perfect storm, and suddenly I found myself free falling, landing with a loud thud into the public stockade. In a fit of self-pity, I probably uttered more than one time, "Can't I get a break?" I received one quite literally with the shattering of my femur, followed by the pulmonary embolism. That break slowed me down enough to reboot and eventually enjoy a more balanced life. Few are given that opportunity.

I came to recognize that being a grand success in the traditional sense is fine—many people do it with grace and dignity. But that was no longer my story, and the earlier I could accept it, the better off I would be. It took a long time for me to realize that my story is just as significant as that of anyone else, albeit different.

We all possess human frailty and we make mistakes. It is vital to prevent being defined by our mistakes or misfortune. While avoiding mistakes is critical, it is also important to "handle" the crucible when it arrives.

As a result of what happened, I began to appreciate more where I had come from and what I could do with the raw material that is me. I recall with humor the flirtations I had experienced with running for office in my former "political" life. I was constantly asked to "throw my hat in the ring." Notably, those same people did not return my phone calls after the "fall." They did not care about my future. How would they know if I was suited for the rough and tumble of politics?

Politics was not my destiny. I did not come from money, knew nothing about how to ask for it, and would have been miserable even trying.

However, I loved the stage and politics has a huge stage. Stages and platforms on which to play out our lives come in many different sizes and scripts.

My grandmother was a quilter—an art that is returning with the turn toward values found in simple human interactions and crafts, which offer a fresh alternative to the bewildering universe. I would marvel as a child at the quilting frame set up in a bedroom of her home in Grassy Creek, Kentucky. While homemade quilts are displayed for sale around the country, those made by my grandmother were special and personal.

I would watch a quilt come together with pieces of clothing that I had worn at last year's family reunion or on the first day of school. The quilts told a story about my grandmother's family, reflecting back to us memories of past days lived and cherished.

As I rebounded physically and mentally from my year of forced contemplation, I embraced the home office that Phoenix and I had considered "confinement" during the months following my accident. I no longer need to be fenced in by the gate that Bernie would erect each morning or by my own sense of failure. Phoenix has grown right by my side. He, too, has moved beyond finding spiritual nourishment in chewing up my shoes. He had moved on to squirrels, rabbits, and birds—more worthy opponents, along with the jiggle machine.

When I open the back door, he flies into the yard like a rock from a tight slingshot. Unlike shoes, squirrels are too clever to be caught, which gives Phoenix the satisfaction of a worthy opponent. Though victory eludes him day after day, he has never lost his zeal for the chase. He relishes the journey. Who said we couldn't learn from dogs?

Though my cane, wheelchair, and walker are history, Phoenix continues to find pleasure in my "reacher," an ingenious device sold to me in the hospital to do just what it implies—reach. The reacher is essentially a stick with a "pincher" on the end. While still constrained in my movements, I found that reaching for the simplest of things was cause for major mental breakdowns. It comes in handy to this day because I am only five-feet, two-inches tall.

Could it be that the reacher is symbolic of my life today—reaching beyond what I was to what I can be, and realizing that my success is measured not by how many likes I receive on Facebook, but my own personal sense of accomplishment?

However, my road has not been on a straight and narrow path. As I regained my health, I continued to troll for speaking engagements and was writing nearly every day. Occasionally, I would hear of something that struck my fancy, such as running a small nonprofit or helping an organization with raising money. I was met with a steady stream of rejections.

As I looked around for something that might be a good fit, I offered to take over an organization whose mission fit me like a glove. The mission was visionary, like its founder. He took on nursing-home reform and has made an immense impact by providing much-needed advocacy. I had experienced firsthand my father's failing health, along with an increased awareness that we were neglecting one of the biggest issues of our time—the care of the aging population.

I offered to assist in any way that I could. I grew excited just thinking about it. I fantasized: I would run the organization, raise the funds that could take it to a new level, and transfer my passion for small cities into this cause—all at no pay. When he approached his board, my press clippings were my undoing. That struck me as a waste of talent and energy. I sobbed for a moment, but for a shorter time with each successive rejection.

I discovered that landing speaking engagements would go very well on the "pitching" side. I would then find that my calls were not returned. Slowly it dawned me what was happening—my prospective suitors were doing what anyone else would do. They were Googling me, and they did not like what they saw. I was also a woman of a "certain age," and that presented obstacles, too.

In the fall of 2010, I seized upon what I thought to be a way forward, using my story by developing my COMPASS speech. I remained obsessed with telling my story—in part to understand it better, and in part to help others benefit from its lessons. I read every article and book I could get my hands on that dealt with crisis management. I became a student of what I believed to be the core needs of boards and leaders in the changing world of today, and assigned a lesson to each letter of the word COMPASS. Of course, the overriding impact was that it would take a compass to allow safe passage through the storms of life.

I read and reread *Crisis Management: Planning for the Inevitable*, by Steven Fink, which is the Bible of the crisis-management books. He provides analysis of the handling of the major high-profile disasters of our times, including the Three Mile Island nuclear meltdown, Tylenol tampering, and others.

His many examples display the difficulty encountered in handling disaster, especially in the early days of social media. We had entered into an era when those in charge—who were publicly exposed—had to accept responsibility, provide authentic compassion (but only if authentic), and put a public face on the tragedy.

Probably the most famous study of reaction to disaster was that of Union Carbide and the 3,787 deaths that resulted from a poisonous gas leak, in 1984, in Bhopal, India. With the recent death of W. M. Anderson, at the age of ninety-two—who held the top job at Union Carbide at the time of the tragedy—the memory of one of history's most lethal industrial accidents surfaced once again. Accused of negligence, Mr. Anderson was the object of scorn by the Indian public, and his safety was compromised the rest of his life.

Five months following the tragedy, Mr. Anderson is quoted as saying: "You wake up in the morning thinking, can it have occurred. And then you know it has, and you know it's something you're going to have to struggle with for a long time."[23] He expressed a desire to find good out of the horror by supporting new industry safety procedures. While it is unclear whether he played a role in moving those reforms forward—perhaps due to cautionary measures that forced him to live almost reclusively—safety procedures have been adopted that continue to be refined.

Like Mr. Anderson, or the doctor who recovered from drug addiction to build a new career running a medical clinic, I immediately thought that—by developing my COMPASS speech—I could help others on a smaller scale to face the crucible and do a better job than I had done. How better to help than with the points of a compass as symbols of the way forward? I hired a public relations firm to help me formulate a presentation. It was the precursor to today's formula of 4Ps (Purpose, Preparation, Planning, and Perspective), which I like much better.

In a triumphant moment, I landed a workshop at the International Institute of Municipal Clerks in Nashville. This was a natural audience for me. Clerks are the salt of the earth— particularly in small towns where they are the often steady hand in the face of democracy, which can produce a new mayor every two to four years through the election cycle. I had developed a great relationship with my Kentucky clerks and hoped for the best before this broader audience.

---

[23] *New York Times* article, "Warren Anderson, 92, Dies; Faced India Plant Disaster"; Douglas, Martin; October 30, 2014.

The presentation appeared to be a hit. The room was packed, and all appeared to go well. After the presentation, I published an article in the IIMC newsletter, as well as in other trade publications. Thinking I would obtain additional opportunities based on my success, I contacted IIMC to propose a follow-up workshop. I received no return phone call, despite several attempts.

In an act of self-preservation, I quickly abandoned the COMPASS speech, along with writing articles about crisis management. I decided that moving on had an even broader meaning, at least for the near future. I was to open a new chapter in my life.

In an unexpected turn, I found myself in the restaurant and food business. It started out as a hobby but became a more serious endeavor following my crucible. I discovered that a dormant entrepreneurial spirit purred under my "hood." Bernie and I are not foodies, as defined by our son Ross, who—as a scientist—often shares unpleasant truths about the origins of our food.

Bernie and I are eaters, but mostly when someone like Chef Jeremy Ashby cooks. And, like most busy people, while I deeply care about food safety and health; conserving food; and eating in moderation, I am not obsessed with food or its origins within the broader margins of safety.

Neither Bernie nor I had restaurant experience, except for being serial in our approach to dining—that meant eating out frequently. We especially loved Roy and Nadine's, a restaurant near our subdivision. I often joke that our children grew up knowing the pizza-delivery number better their own.

We had first attempted to buy Roy and Nadine's, our favorite diner, but the deal fell through. Instead, we refurbished an insurance office—located in a strip shopping center—and turned it into Azur Restaurant and Patio. Founded in 2006, it has become quite successful.

Azur Restaurant and Patio is an upscale farm-to-table restaurant, which filled a market niche. Today, we are also part owners of another restaurant, Brasabana, which features Cuban cuisine, as well as of Dupree Catering. Brasabana will prove exceptionally fun with the continued and ultimately successful opening up of Cuban culture to Americans.

Much lies beneath the surface in our love of restaurants that relates to who we are. Bernie and I found fulfillment in something deeper inside each of us than just the food. As we look into the dining rooms of our restaurants, Bernie, with his love of literature, and me, as a story collector, were struck by the stories that each guest brings in the door.

People break bread with one another for various reasons—to mourn, to celebrate, to laugh, and to cry. Breaking "bread" presents an opportunity to bond with one another in a world that is increasingly devoid of such opportunities. As with my beloved mayors, I find myself wanting to approach each customer with a camcorder to record every story.

The evening that my mother died is seared in my memory and connects with our love of food and restaurants. Those who so loved her held her hand and our collective breath as she gasped her last ones on December 19, 2001. There we were—my father, me, Bernie, Ross, David, and her caregiver—gathered around her hospital bed that had long taken the place of her dining room table.

Her favorite sister, Aunt Ruth, who was particularly spiritual—had just rushed in after a three-hour drive from Ohio following our pleas that she come and "give my mother permission" to go. We had tried a telephone call from Ruth, but my mother would have none of it. We begged her to give in and let go in those final agonizing hours; she refused, instead gasping and struggling to stay alive.

I will never forget my anxiety as Ruth's car came into the driveway, and her taillights went out. She ran up the steps, into the house, and around the bed to where my mother's head was cocked. "It's okay," she said, as she stooped toward my mother's face. "You can go now and see Mom and Dad in heaven."

At that point, it was as if the room was filled with the "Hallelujah" chorus from Handel's Messiah. We collectively screamed as my mom finally gasped three times and passed into sudden peace. Unlike Ruth, my mother was not spiritual and feared death, which made her illness even sadder and her letting go even harder.

People who have watched the ravages of cancer drain the life from a loved one will know what I mean when I say that her death was a blessing. They understand how profound suffering can suddenly turn into inexplicable, but welcomed, peace in an instant for the loved one and all those who love her.

After she was taken away, I suggested to Bernie that we get a drink at Roy and Nadine's Restaurant. We bellied up to the bar and sipped our drinks as the barkeeper scurried about. I feared that he might ask how my day went. My reply would have been an uncomfortable, "We are celebrating the passing of my mother." I have learned that people "celebrate" many things over food.

We love the restaurant business, despite its many challenges. Since our shared crucible, we have become even more engaged. I often joke that the restaurant idea arose out of Bernie's midlife crisis. I tell him, "it is cheaper than a woman half my age, but may be more expensive."

One cold evening in January 2012, Chef Jeremy— who had returned to being a full-time chef (after retiring from his role of walking Phoenix, of course)— approached Bernie and me about an offer from a local radio station. The station had offered Jeremy a one-hour radio program about food.

He lamented his lack of time and inexperience with media. Without hesitation, I replied, "Say yes. We'll do it together!" Before my disaster, I had done on-air op-eds for the local public radio station, in addition to written pieces published all over the world. My public radio "career" had come to an end when the station manager suggested that what happened to me made that a bad idea— no doubt for him. He wanted no part of me. My radio venture with Chef Jeremy continues with Food News and Chews radio.

I am involved with all aspects of the show from writing the scripts, to researching food news, to recruiting guests. Given my background in policy, I research "food news," both fun and serious. We feature segments like Food in the Movies; Restaurant Rumors; The Weirdest Reason I ever went to a Restaurant; Stuff that is not supposed to be in Stuff, But is in Stuff, and more. With Jeremy's rising fame as a chef, an important element on every show is his mouthwatering description of each dish in delectable detail—we called this food porn.

My shtick on the show has always been channeling as best I can, within the limits of my inferior talent, the memory of Lucille Ball of I Love Lucy fame. It was as if I was reliving the talent portion of the Miss MSU Pageant all over again. It is liberating. This time, my age was an advantage. Like a younger Betty White—the 90-plus-year-old actress, who has found fame late in life—I could get by with such antics as teasing Jeremy and Twitch, our other co-host, and making provocative statements and flirtations.

Our show's mission is educating our listeners about the bewildering world of the local food movement. In my case, I want listeners to look beyond food and see its symbolic role in our quest for meaning. That is what juices me up—always looking for the broad strokes of what appears to be ordinary aspects of our lives. Our listeners are likely harried and busy. They are seeking something in food, though, that is important to their well-being, which may be defined as better health—or even spiritual grounding—with the words "natural," "local," and "fresh."

In preparation for each show, I put myself in the shoes of a typical rushed, time-starved consumer. How does it feel for him or her to walk into a restaurant or a supermarket and be bombarded with food touted to have been grown organically, conventionally, or from heirloom seeds? "So, what is the difference?" is a natural response.

I relish the opportunity to speak to the noon Rotary Club luncheons, filled with serious executives and women who would steadfastly deny interest in the local food movement. I start with a quiz. I instruct my audience that an affirmative answer to my question qualifies one as a "foodie."

I ask the question, "Who in this room likes to eat?" All hands rise with a resounding "yes," and all are declared foodies. I share with them the practical advantages of paying attention to the local food movement with its implications for safety, access, and conservation in a country that wastes forty percent of its food. I talk about building a local economy that supports "local" stores, restaurants, and producers. I grab their attention and interest with the quiz. They leave far more interested than when they arrived.

And then, I always return to my beloved food radio. Radio allows listeners freedom and creativity. What better way to create the picture than through mouthwatering descriptions of food? Keeping with my shtick, my trademark apron worn at events reads: "So I'm not Betty

Crocker; deal with it." I love this apron and I am eternally grateful to the Mill City Museum in Minneapolis, Minnesota, where I fell in love with it. (There really is a flour museum paying tribute to the flour industry of Minnesota—think wheat fields—it is wonderful.)

With all that was going on to turn my life around by getting well and steeping myself in the restaurant business, I had been united with Mike Gobb at Alan Stein's consulting group, SteinGroup—and little did I know that our lives would become intertwined yet again.

CHAPTER FOURTEEN

The Loss of Mike

"You have to go to the bottom to truly see the top."

—Mike Gobb

Mike Gobb's suicide, in September 2013, was the crucible that led me to write these stories. Mike and I were reunited when Alan Stein invited both of us to be part of his consulting company. Until then, I relied only on Bernie's reports about Mike and the fits and starts that made up his attempt to reclaim his life.

I am blessed to have known Mike. His story informed my own. What others think of me has become less important and I find great joy in small activities. I have written this book as a way to honor my dear friend Mike by doing what I hoped he would have done after his reputation disaster, recover and share the learning lessons that he, Bernie, and I were uniquely given.

Elizabeth Kubler-Ross made famous the "five stages of grief," originally about coming to accept the diagnosis of a fatal illness. According to her, the five stages of grief are denial, anger, bargaining, depression, and finally acceptance. [24] The "five stages" model has since been adapted to encompass all events that induce grief. Someone once said, "Grief doesn't change you; it just makes you more of who you are."

I lived and felt a similar journey. I grieved for my lost job and my lost life. I can attest to the authentic grip of grief on me at various times. Even today, acceptance will sometimes lose its way, especially in the darkness of night when the demons return.

As the saying goes, one person can throw a pebble in a pond and it takes a thousand geniuses to stop the ripples. I am not a genius, but I am happy to report that the ripples are subsiding and that I take each one as it comes, by relying on my formula. I know that my Purpose is worthwhile and important; I prepare every day to understand my world better; plan my life accordingly; and finally, recognize the perspective and importance of leadership.

Mike went on one last vacation to the Grand Canyon just a month before he died. It turns out Mike lied when he told us that the primary purpose of his trip to the Southwest was to visit airports for consulting work.

In letters delivered posthumously, we discovered that the real objective of his trip was never visiting airports, but that one last vacation to the Grand Canyon.

---

[24] *On Death and Dying* by Dr. Elizabeth Kubler-Ross; 1997.

He described the visit as exhilarating—a place where he found new friends and inspiration. Mike explained that he returned at peace with his decision to end his life. He described the importance of the trip that took him to the bottom of that magnificent place.

What was Mike's message? "You have to go to the bottom to truly see the top." Mike had symbolically reached the bottom of the Grand Canyon of his life.

Years earlier, during his recovery from drug addiction, Mike had gained a deep faith. When he was found, Sarah Young's book, *Jesus Calling*, lay beside him. My question, and perhaps yours, is: "Did Mike really reach the top?" On the one hand, I have no right to question his decision or stand in judgment, but I do, and I am angry with him. If he were still with us, I'd scold him and hug him with all my heart and soul.

I am angry about all the wasted talent and all the good he could have done. I am sad that he never shared the lessons he had learned. He had chosen to concentrate on reclaiming his old life, which was gone, rather than begin again, wiser, less judgmental, and more compassionate. Had he chosen that path, I believe he would have healed himself in the process. Mike never let go of the past, and because of that decision, the past never let go of him.

My suspicion is that Mike was guilty of not forgiving, perhaps the most important component of humility. With the exception of Alan Stein, Bernie, and a handful of others, he found no forgiveness in his community.

More profoundly, I believe that he could not forgive himself.

Mike could have left the toxic environment of central Kentucky. He could have started an entirely new story just about anywhere. However, instead, he gave up. He should have realized the impossibility of erasing even a bit of your life story. It is better to weave the weak strands of pain and mistakes into your life's tapestry, than to pre- tend that the damage is not there. The most expensive oriental rug is not the new one, but the one that has aged, is flawed, imperfect, but rich with the stories of its history, mapped out in the frayed edges, and worn patterns.

Enduring dark nights in the hospital, I pondered forgiveness as perhaps the most noble of human traits. Forgiveness involves acquiring the humility to understand your imperfections and those of others, and still having the will to get up each day and do better. It is about the humor that often eases the pain of life's tragic moments. Moreover, finally, it is about having the hutzpah in the midst of chaos to lead and provide the inspiration that is missing in today's world. It is about the paradox of realizing that we may be insignificant to the vast universe in one way, yet incredibly significant to those we can help along the way.

During one of those special moments, I was enjoying coffee conversation with a friend. We were talking about our tiny stake in the grand universe. Neither of us was going to broker world peace, run for president, have buildings named for us, or be the subject of historians pondering our every decision. We suddenly grew silent and then—almost simultaneously—recalled the ones who made a difference not only in our own lives, but also in those of others. They were not well-known people. Teachers came easily to mind.

We ended the conversation with the thought that—perhaps like a teacher—somewhere along the way, each of us made a difference in someone's life. Someone who we have touched may do a grand thing in the world—impacting it in a positive way or doing something profound, like teaching young children or helping the elderly as a volunteer. We may not even be privy to ever knowing that person's good works because such an individual is not a celebrity. That was enough to leave us satisfied and grateful.

I think of the story about two people walking along the shore, when they encounter a sand dollar drying in the sun. One of the two companions retrieves the sand dollar and throws it back into the ocean. The second companion comments, "Why did you bother to throw it back in the water. It is only one sand dollar, and you cannot save them all. In the larger scheme of things, it doesn't make a difference."

"It makes a difference to this one," said the companion. "It makes a difference to this one."

How I wish Mike could have embraced forgiveness of himself and had the hutzpah to soldier on. He had much to share, and—now that he is gone—it is for me and for others who knew him to tell his story and, by so doing, help others to redemption.

I have become good friends with Eric Frankl, who was hired to replace Mike in the aftermath of the airport disaster. He has been quite successful getting the airport restored to its former glory. Eric, a wise leader, could have boasted about his work in restoring the airport's reputation. He could have assigned blame to the board or to Mike. Instead, he did something extraordinary.

He became Mike's good friend, treating him regularly to coffee and conversation about how to gain a toehold on his life. That took humility, and it took hutzpah. He had the courage to understand his own set of responsibilities, but the confidence to reach out to Mike, who had so sadly lost his way.

At the luncheon hosted by my good friends in the fall of 2009, in the midst of my flying coconuts, I was given a special gift of *Short of the Glory: The Fall and Redemption of Edward F. Prichard Jr.*, Tracy Campbell's biography of the man known as "Prich." He was a wunderkind—a prodigy—who, from his birth in Paris, Kentucky, in 1915, in the heart of bourbon and horse country, was destined to be successful ... until he was not.

Gifted with a photographic memory and sharp wit, he graduated at the top of his class at Princeton University and Harvard Law School. He held important inner-circle posts in the Roosevelt and Truman administrations. He ultimately served as a clerk in the U.S. Supreme Court before returning to Kentucky to assume his rightful place—widely defined as a choice of running either for governor or for the U.S. Senate.

Falling victim to ego and hubris, he was convicted of stuffing 254 ballots in a U.S. Senate race in his hometown in Bourbon County—not an uncommon offense in Kentucky in those days, or some might say even now. Prich, in all his brilliance—or because of it—possessed an arrogance that made enemies.

He inspired the ire of J. Edgar Hoover, who was the founder and first director of the Federal Bureau of Investigation (FBI) during the Roosevelt administration. Though others may have been guilty of such transgressions, Prich was singled-out, prosecuted, and convicted. He was sentenced to five months in jail before President Truman pardoned him.

Leaving prison in deep shame and having lost his law license, he spent the next twenty-five years longing for a return to his old life. He was no longer touted for elected office. Even though he was a gifted orator, the high profile and the stage were gone. With his intellect undimmed by the bitter experience, and his law license restored, he eventually rebuilt his law practice.

Prich reemerged as a prized behind-the-scenes adviser to governors and legislators. However, that was not the ultimate and most important story of his redemption. During the seventies and eighties, before his death in 1984 at the age of sixty-nine, Prich became an eloquent and cogent voice for education reform—demanding that all children be given equal opportunities for a quality education in a poor state, which had for too long neglected the educational needs of its citizens. He founded, and lent his name to, the Prichard Committee for Academic Excellence. It remains active today and has been a driving force for reforms that have transformed Kentucky's education system.

Though Prich no doubt would have preferred his original script and could have coasted to a glorious political career, it is widely believed that his greater contribution is as the champion of education reform, rather than as a governor or as a senator. In a model replicated throughout the world, Prich's redemption exemplifies his political prowess. His work allowed many children, then and today, to receive a higher quality of education because of his post-disaster crusade.

Late in his life, he became the subject of press attention, interviews, and documentaries, exploring the reason he threw away his reputation for 254 ballots. In one revealing interview with William Buckley, he observed, "I think you find moral complexities, moral ambiguities, antimonies, in the greatest of leaders …. All have sinned and come short of the glory of God, and I don't deny it for a minute."

I recall being delighted at receiving Prich's biography. Knowing he had served time in jail, I was alarmed. Did my friends believe I deserve jail time? No doubt reading my body language, the group assured me that "while this story isn't exactly yours, we wanted you to see that reinvention is possible … at any age." In Prich's case, he not only overcame a reputation disaster, but battled debilitating diabetes that eventually led to blindness.

No doubt—as Mike felt and Prich likely felt at the beginning of their crucibles—I just wanted my old life back, and nothing less would make me happy. I had had a great job and had built a strong and prosperous organization that helped people. Why couldn't all this go away and I have my old life back?

I found Prich's story to be a page-turner that spoke to my heart—a story of a great and remarkable man, who was Phoenix rising out of ashes—and I thought of Mike, Bernie, and me. All of us were the focus of adoration before the fall. We received many awards and accolades. I was "Appalachian Woman of the Year," "Public Official of the Year," and more. Mike and Bernie, too, received numerous accolades. One headline featured a laudatory article about me that screamed, "League of her own— League of Cities director named to associations (National Association of Women Business Owners—NAWBO) Winner's Circle." It was flattering, but it had little value to me or to anyone else after my fall.

I finally and humbly identified with Prich. In fact— though I am not his equal in intellect or fame, and I did not commit a criminal act—I welcome comparisons to him far more than to those adorned with the more traditional attributes of success.

I only wish that Mike could have known more about Prich and could have followed his path to redemption. He was unforgiven by his community. He had enormous gifts and could have made a difference in so many lives, as did Prich.

Epilogue

Finding My Inner Subaru

At one time, I had eighty staff members at my disposal. I drove a very nice car. I was riding high, and then it all crashed. Today, I am an author, have my restaurant and consulting businesses. Some have told me that I run a risk of bringing up all the "bad stuff" again with this book. They caution me; "all is nearly forgotten." I am compelled, however, to tell the story on Mike's behalf. Besides, I do drive a Subaru Outback. The car that is so ugly it is cute. In addition, it is "durable" and "rough around the edges"—the acknowledged new me.

I have a handful of trusted advisers, including my beloved Freda, who served as my executive assistant for ten years. Phoenix, the puppy who shepherded me through the recovery from my femur break, is now nearing doggie middle age. He is my chief of staff. I still own the Azur Restaurant and Patio and Brasabana restaurants, along with my husband and three other partners. I still do radio with Chef Jeremy Ashby.

I work with the restaurants in many ways and harbor a desire to spin off a coffee shop, where I can engage in the quieter conversations that can only come with relaxing over coffee or tea. I have greeted tables and bussed away the dishes. I find it rewarding to have enough confidence to do just about anything that allows me to better pursue my strong sense of curiosity.

At one time, in a pinch, I served customers. My standard line was, "They don't let me carry more than two waters at a time, and Chef Miguel never, ever lets me in the kitchen!" I add, "And, I am damn good at cleaning off tables—it's about time that law degree paid off."

I lead an active and full life, grounded in my Purpose. I speak to groups; conduct leadership seminars and board retreats; and passionately pursue my calling, which helps companies and the people working there find their way in a bewildering world. I often challenge my audiences to "go ahead and make my day—Google me."

I deny no part of my story. It makes up the fabric of my life as surely as does any other part. As I often tease, "No one can say that I haven't lived an interesting life."

One reporter, while scolding me—post-crucible—observed with no doubt a puffed-up ego, "As a journalist, I am taught to question everything." I quietly demurred. I knew that, to the contrary, he did not question enough. He was not curious, or he would have delved into the stories of Mike, Bernie, and me; shed light on the nuances and threads of what was happening to all of us; and allowed his readers a glimpse into their own lives that only good writing and journalism can bring.

Time has softened the edges. It is hard to figure out any science to reactions that I have received. I had lunch recently with a very successful woman executive, who has become a good friend and mentor. She told me how her ninety-year-old mother-in-law was angry after reading the negative coverage I received. "It's not fair," she said.

The only sense I can make of all the reactions is an observation that we live in an era that has spawned fragmented and diverse opinions on just about anything. Because of social media, those opinions are accepted and expressed publicly. The coconuts are flying and threaten to throw us off-center at every moment.

I find myself gravitating to strong women as role models—women like Freda Meriwether, my former executive assistant; Marchetta Sparrow, former Kentucky Secretary of Tourism; and Linda Hollembaek, who travels the world. One particularly welcoming person who has changed my life is Judy Clabes, a famed and inspirational presence in the media world.

Not giving into retirement, she is the founding mother of many endeavors, including www.KyForward.com, an online newspaper. She is courageous, visionary, and tireless in her pursuit to bring important stories to her readers and find ways to serve those in need. I could follow her around anywhere just to soak up her energy and can-do attitude. She is among the curious, who is willing to turn up every stone in an effort to tell the full story.

I volunteered to assist her in a troubled elementary school as she instructed the students to put together a school newspaper. That has been quite an experience. I pinch myself at my good fortune of being asked to even stand in the same room with Judy.

Volunteering in the school was a departure from my past, when I had served on high-profile boards and commissions. I was a part of the development and shaping of major policies. I am unsure that I made much of a difference because those same committees and commissions are debating the same issues today. Because of that high-profile service, though, I likely received awards and praise I did not deserve. I find that I would rather make a smaller difference, albeit unheralded, by working directly with those in need. I will leave world peace and boiling the ocean to others. I will take it on a teaspoon at a time.

During my first session with the elementary class, Judy introduced me as "famous" and went on to describe my past work running KLC, which she described as a vital statewide organization. I cringed as I heard the word "famous." I wanted to protest, but before I could do so, the moment was transformed when one particularly vocal young fifth-grader shouted out in the middle of the introduction about what a great thing it is to be in the presence of someone famous. "She can get any man she wants!" he observed. Again, humor can break tension.

As I design and conduct workshops, I continue my obsession with the stories about those who failed, but were able to dust themselves off and get back in the game. We all love the stories of overcomers. Often, after

I have spoken, someone will share a story that is similar to mine.

I encourage them to write their story and use it to help others. They express a desire to learn how to avoid, and ultimately handle, disasters. Rather than hear from the award-and-trophy-resume or the Photoshopped speakers, they want an authentic story that reveals the true journey to growth, along with all the bumps in the road.

We must rejoice in, and embrace, our unique stories. My son once lived in Duluth, Minnesota, located on the shores of Lake Superior. Typical winter temperatures are in the single digits and below. Being more of a warm-weather fan, I particularly dreaded visits in the winter. Working through my crucibles, however, I came to find strength in visiting northern Minnesota. Now that my son has left Duluth, I miss it. The ruggedness in the people and their commitment to place and to one another are enviable.

When a friend tells me about heading for Naples, Florida—if not Italy—for a January respite, I proudly and truthfully announce my intentions to visit Duluth and the magnificent Lake Superior. I love the looks I get that shout, "Are you crazy?"

Nothing restores my soul like the chilly walk along Lake Superior's shores. I gaze out at that vast expanse of water, often in subzero temperatures, and marvel at the turns in my life that I did not anticipate or even want. I think of the stories it yields from the many ships, anglers,

and others—who plied their trades in and on its waters—
and even those who now lie at its bottom.

Lake Superior's grand expanse and power are humbling, and inspire me to rejoice in the time I have—to be
with family and friends and make a difference in someone's life. I typically leave my conversation partner un-
convinced, but that is okay. Who else gets a chance to
walk on water as I did, during January 2014, when Lake
Superior froze over for the first time in thirty years?

I have lived a charmed life. I will use as the foundation what I have learned, not only from my story, but
also from Mike's and Bernie's.

In Summary

I have learned to take the old airline adage to heart:
"Put your own mask on first before helping others." I
have learned to embrace myself before I can begin to assist others in significant ways. This is not a narcissistic
statement—we all are more like Prich than we are willing
to admit. We are flawed. We can still vow to do better.

I have learned that, like medical checkups, we must
regularly assess and support our mental and spiritual well-
being with a variety of "self-care" techniques. By so doing, we are better prepared for the inevitable crucible that
will come our way.

As a unique individual, I have my gifts and weaknesses, as we all do. Learning to shore up the weaknesses
and play to strengths is important. I could not have imagined or written my life story in advance. It has been full
of surprises, and above all, unique and beautiful. I have

been blessed to know so many special people and expect to know many more.

I end with a thought as expressed by Sully, of *Miracle on the Hudson* fame. Darren Hardy, publisher of SUC-CESS magazine, asked him to explain the next step in his illustrious career as one of the most prominent public faces of leadership.

Sully's fame is grounded in landing a jetliner full of passengers on the Hudson River, an act akin to walking on the moon. I was taken aback by his response. "I live my life as if my greatest contribution is yet to come."

It was an incredible answer. I humbly vow no less to look to the future for even greater moments of service and contribution.

About Sylvia Lovely

Sylvia Lovely is an author, speaker, and motivator–helping leaders achieve resiliency and success in work and play through her unique approach called "Dodging Coconuts." In keynotes, workshops, and coaching sessions, she frames her "lessons learned" using her 4P Process: (1) Purpose – required to manage the micro and macro forces raging about us; (2) Preparation – understanding the mission of work and life; (3) Planning and (4) Perspective of Leadership–developing the foundations of leadership. All this is done within the frame and context of relentless change and the "information blitzkrieg" that defines 21st century work and life. Her audiences range from individual leaders to governing boards and mid and senior-level business managers.

In her recently published book, Dodging Coconuts: How to Survive the Storm and Rebuild Your Life, she shares both her story and valuable lessons she has learned from her personal and professional experiences to help individuals and companies achieve their goals. She emphasizes how our personal well-being is increasingly intertwined with our professional lives. She is dedicated to helping others become effective, willing, and bold decision-makers in spite of a widespread sense of bewilderment about life in our modern era.

Sylvia brings to her work 22 years of experience as CEO of the Kentucky League of Cities. (An association of 380 city members in Kentucky with a $54 million dollar annual budget.), her training as an attorney, and her experience as a national speaker and author. She has authored two other books, which reveal her interest in the human dynamic of "community interaction." Those books are *The Little Blue Book of Big Ideas – New Cities in America* and *The Little Red Book of Everyday Heroes*.

Sylvia has served on many boards including as chair of the Morehead State University Board of Regents, her alma mater located in the heart of Appalachia. She brings to her work her life experiences beginning with her parents' humble beginnings in Appalachia to Dayton, Ohio where they escaped the poverty of small town, rural Kentucky. She encourages others to embrace their life story for the enriching contributions all our experiences bring to our lives.

Today, Sylvia is an entrepreneur and part owner of Azur Food Group (AFG), consisting of Azur Restaurant and Patio, Brasabana Restaurant featuring Cuban cuisine, and Dupree Catering and Events, one of the largest regional catering companies in central Kentucky. She and her AFG co-owner, Chef Jeremy Ashby, co-host Food News and Chews, a popular radio program which educates listeners about food and the local food movement.

She lives in Lexington with husband Bernie and her dog Phoenix. She enjoys her children, David and Lauren Lovely and Jennifer and Ross Lovely, and grandchildren Jack Levi, Mary Simon and a granddaughter due to arrive in August.

"My goal is to help you engage in the highest order of leadership by embracing what is ultimately YOUR story in both work and play."

—Sylvia Lovely

Bibliography

Dramatists Play Service Inc., (1953); "The Crucible", Miller, Arthur, published 1982.

Stephen Crane, Sir, I exist (1899, in a compilation, "War is Kind and Other Poems", published June 19, 1998)

National Cash Register Corporation, "NCR producing a peak 110,000 cash registers in one year alone"; http://www.ohiohistorycentral.org/w/National_Cash_Register Company

"Revival" Album; Annabelle; Welch, Gilliam, April 9, 1996.

"The Harlem Renaissance", britannica.com.

"Their Eyes were watching God"; Hurston, Zora Neale, A Novel Reissue Edition; Harper Perennial Modern Classics, www.thegreatestbooks.com, 2003.

Lexington Herald Leader, "Gobb's service: Ex-airport chief made valuable contributions", Perry, David, September 18, 2013.

Lexington Herald Leader; "Pilot error blamed in plane crash that killed 49"; Ortiz, Brandon, Patton, Janet, Ku Michelle; July 27, 2007.

Lexington Herald Leader; "Year Later, Sense of Loss Remains Strong – 1600 Attend Service Honoring 49 who died in crash one year ago; Mead, Andy, Honeycutt, Valerie, August 27, 2007.

Lexington Herald Leader; "A Sky High Expense Account-It's worth it, board chair says"; Hewlett, Jennifer, November 23, 2008.

Lexington Herald Leader; "Airport paid tab at Texas strip club – Credit cards canceled after $4500 visit comes to light"; Hewlett, Jennifer and Alessi, Ryan, January 6, 2009.

Lexington Herald Leader; "Council Ask Chair to Step Down – Newberry Criticizes Preliminary Vote"; *Ku, Michelle,* January 7, 2009.

Lexington Herald Leader; "Ex-airport director Gobb pleads guilty —Admits to 2 counts of felony theft by deception in plea bargain"; Hewlett, Jennifer; June 19, 2010.

Lexington Herald Leader; "Gobb steps down, Resignation immediate no severance new questions involve use of other's credit cards"; Hewlett, Jennifer, January 3, 2009.

Lexington Herald Leader; "Ex-airport chief gets probation sentence includes drug testing, community service - Judge cites substance abuse, lack of criminal record"; Hewlett, Jennifer, August 14, 2010.

The Little Red Book of Everyday Herooes; Page 103; Lovely, Sylvia; The Clark Group, September 9, 2007; Lexington, Kentucky.

The Little Blue Book of Big Ideas; Lovely, Sylvia; Minerva Publishing; 2004; Louisville, Kentucky.

Lexington Herald Leader; "League prospers as Ky cities struggle mayor asks for review of salaries Non-profit's execs get big raises, perks"; Blackford, Linda; June 7, 2009.

Lexington Herald Leader; "League of Cities tightens ethics—New rules include it's first-ever conflict-of-interest guidelines" Blackford, Linda, August 20, 2009.

Lexington Herald Leader; "KLC: a mess of conflicts, excess - Board seems clueless to wastefulness"; Commentary, December 17, 2009.

Seven Storey Mountain; Merton, Thomas; 1948 - Mariner Books; Anv edition (October 4, 1999).

Lexington Herald Leader; "Tragic turns in Life, death raise questions on what's 'significant'; Lovely, Sylvia L.; January 27, 2012.

"Don't come back from Hell Empty handed," Mackoff, Barbra; Wiley, John & Son Publishers, January 13, 2009.

"MDNG Pain Management"; Falling Down, Dove, Alan, PhD, January 23, 2009.

Highest Duty: My Search for What Really Matters; Sullenberger, Chesley B. and Zaslow, Jeffrey; William Morrow—1 Edition, October 13, 2009.

When Bad Things Happen to Good People; Kushner, Harold S.; Anchor, 1978, Reprint Edition August 24, 2004, pg. 147.

Please Understand Me: Character and Temperament Types; Keirsey, David and Bates, Marilyn; Prometheus Nemesis Book Company; 5th edition (January 1, 1984).

"Generation Flux's Secret Weapon"; Safian, Robert; *Fast Company*- November, 2014.

Bowling Alone: The Collapse and Revival of American Community; Putman, Robert D.; Touchstone Books by Simon & Schuster; 1st edition (August 7, 2001).

Organization Man; Whyte, William H.; Doubleday Anchor Books, January 1, 1957.

"Bob Dole Looks Back"; Green, Charles; AARP Bulletin; Vol. 56, No. 6; July/August, 2015.

"Mindfulness";
www.psychologytoday.com/basics/mindfulness.

"Meditation"; www.medicinenewstoday.com_– February 26, 2014.

"Business as a Movement"; Eileen Fisher; Safain, Robert; *Fast Company* Magazine; November 2014.

Take Good Care of the Garden and the Dogs: A True Story of Bad Breaks and Small Miracles; Lende, Heather; Algonquin Books; April 19, 2011.

One Summer: America 1927; Bryson, Bill; Anchor; Reprint edition June 3, 2014.

Fifty Shades of Grey; James E. L. Vintage; May 25, 2011.

Learning to Walk in the Dark; Taylor, Barbara Brown; Harper One; Reprint edition (April 8, 2014).

"How Unethical Behavior Becomes Habit"; Gino, Francesca, Ordonez, Lisa D. and Welsh, David; Harvard Business Review, September 4, 2014.

"Send in the Clowns"; Judy Collins, Sondheim, Stephen, Chappell; 1973.

Crisis Management: Planning for the Inevitable; Fink, Steven; iUniverse; June 19, 2000. (1986 and 2002).

New York Times; "Warren Anderson, 92, Dies, Faced India Plant Disaster; Martin", Douglas; October 30, 2014.

On Death and Dying; Ross, Elizabeth Kubler; Scribner; Reprint edition June 9, 1997.

Jesus Calling: Enjoying Peace in His Presence; Young, Sarah; Thomas Nelson; Special and Rev Edition October 12, 2004.

Short of the Glory, the Fall and Redemption of Edward F. Prichard; Campbell, Tracy; University Press of Kentucky; October 15, 2004, 2 Edition (October 15, 2004).

Lexington Herald Leader; League of Her Own - League of Cities Director Named to Association's Winner's Circle; Brim, Rism; May 6, 2003.

.